HIGHLAND IN LMS DAYS
David Jenkinson

D1644471

CONTENTS

A characteristic LMS scene on the Highland main line in April 1931: 'Loch' Class 4-4-0 No.14392 Loch Naver, *still bearing the original pre-1928 LMS red livery, leaving Perth with the 4.00pm 'all stations' to Blair Atholl. The leading carriage is a fairly new LMS standard non-corridor type.* (Author's collection)

INTRODUCTION

The Highland Railway was one of those rare species in the broader British railway story which was almost universally popular amongst almost all enthusiasts, no matter what their other allegiances may have been. It is no part of my brief to try to explain this phenomenon, save to mention it *en passant*, but it is my intention in these pages to try to recount just some part of it, namely that very fascinating 25 year phase between 1923 and 1947 when it moved from being a rather modest part of the broader Scottish railway scene, with all its implied limitations, to its rather more significant role, albeit constantly under threat in context of its longer term survival, as the most northerly outpost of the largest Joint Stock Corporation running railways in any part of the world at the time: the London Midland and Scottish Railway Company of Great Britain (LMS).

Despite repeated talk of closing much of it down from late HR and early LMS days until well into the 1960s and later, the main network somehow managed to stay intact, more or less, into the 21st Century, despite its somewhat marginal economic viability from the very earliest days. That it survived to fulfil an important role in the larger British nationalised system after 1947, and is still doing so in the post-privatisation world of our own time after the great upheavals of the 1990s (written in 2003), is a welcome thought, albeit no part of this particular story. But the fact that the system is still largely extant at all (save for a few relatively insignificant minor branches), some 80 years or more after the original company went into limbo in

1923 - often against the broader national trend for that matter - is certainly worth a passing note and is in large part a result of the the attention it was given during that brief 1923-47 period which we now call 'The Grouping'. This short but vital part of its life is the main theme of this offering.

In it, some of the many features which survived from a very fascinating system during a brief 25 year phase when times were hard but which were to be vital in context, are examined in fair detail, accompanied by many visual images of the ever-changing scene in the Scottish Highlands to be observed at that time - many hitherto unpublished. However, given the limited space available, the author (whose interest was first fired by his good friend the late Gavin Wilson, who died well before his due time in 1976) would never claim it to be a definitive or fully comprehensive presentation of the whole story *per se*; but it is my hope that these pages allow sufficient space to offer some of the essential flavour of a distinctive element of the British railway scene during the last 25 years of genuinely private existence (as opposed to the present day pseudo-private but nationally subsidised situation) and contribute something to our greater understanding of a long gone era.

David Jenkinson
North Yorkshire
December 2003

Typical of the 1920s, Drummond 0-6-4T No.15307 runs through Dalnaspidal on its way back to Blair Atholl, having completed a northbound banking job to Druimuachdar Summit. (The late H.C.Casserley)

1

The LMS Inheritance

IT IS NOT the purpose of this book to record the history of the Highland Railway as such; that is already in print and need not be repeated here (see Bibliography). But, if only for the benefit of those coming new to the scene, it does seem useful to start this survey by way of reviewing the essential background to the LMS situation.

The Highland Railway itself evolved over many years, its eventual system being far different from that which had been envisaged by the promoters of its first important element, a direct main line from Inverness to Perth in 1861 by way of the Inverness and Perth Junction Railway. This line, striking off from Forres (itself on an already existing but circuitous line to the south running mainly north and east of the main mountain massif to Aberdeen), was proposed to go over the harder and more direct route south via Dava, Aviemore, Druimuachdar Summit, Blair Atholl and Pitlochry, eventually to link up at Stanley Junction with the extensive Caledonian Railway (CR) network radiating from Perth.

This line was in no way the first railway to be promoted north of Perth and Aberdeen in those early days, for what later became part of the Great North of Scotland Railway (GNSR) north of Aberdeen via far easier terrain (as mentioned above) was much earlier on the scene as were sundry other lines east of Inverness. But the GNSR never reached Inverness in its own right, having to settle for an end-on junction at Keith with one of these earlier companies, the Inverness and Aberdeen Junction Railway. This route to Aberdeen, where the GNSR itself made an end-on junction with the CR, offered a far longer journey between Inverness and Perth than the new line. *(NB The GNSR also reached Elgin via its own line from Keith via Craigellachie - for system map see outside rear cover)*

History was soon to show that the direct route from Forres was by far the more important link in the broader scheme of things and it soon became the main line to Inverness from the south and the principal stem of the Highland system as later generations were to know it. Indeed, it was the promotion of this shorter route south which caused several companies with an interest in it, to amalgamate under the consolidated name Highland Railway in 1865: but the GNSR remained resolutely aloof....... The advantage which the Highland now held in terms of through traffic to and from the south was made even more significant after the company itself built a shorter cut-off from Inverness to Aviemore via Carr Bridge in 1898. This line, over Slochd Summit and now the only direct rail link north of

Aviemore, shortened the distance by a further 26 miles. But for many years, including the whole of the LMS period, both lines from Aviemore to Inverness were in full use and generally far more convenient than any other offerings.

Meantime, the Highland itself had expanded its system so as to take over the running of two very long but significant routes north of Inverness, namely the 'Far North' line to Wick and Thurso and the cross-country line to the Kyle of Lochalsh, albeit that the latter location was not reached until some few years after most of the route had been opened as far as Strome Ferry in 1870 as the Dingwall and Skye Railway. These lines, always worked by the Highland, were promoted by a variety of different organisations during the 1860s and 1870s but the HR itself took over the Skye line in 1880 and built the extension from Strome Ferry in 1897. The Far North lines, independently promoted by three separate companies between 1868 and 1874, but again worked by the Highland, were taken over in 1884. Diverging just north of Dingwall, these two long, circuitous and generally remote routes have always been of major interest to enthusiasts and it is most pleasing to note that both of them still survive as this account is written in 2003.

Well before the grouping, however, the Highland had also built several smaller branches from its main arteries as the system developed and thus it was when the LMS took over. In essence, the trunk of the system ran from Perth to Inverness, with its two alternative routes to the latter location north of Aviemore, together with the two principal and very long routes north and west of Inverness and all the associated branches and minor lines both from the main routes themselves and to the east of the Highland Capital. Its geographical coverage, albeit wide, was very well defined and, save for a few places in the east where it met the GNSR, it enjoyed a total territorial monopoly - anything else would have been financial disaster!

Just why the Highland was finally subsumed into the LMS is not fully known to this writer, who has been quite unable to discover all the precise reasons which underlined the final division of the main pre-group Scottish companies between the LMS and LNER (London and North Eastern Railway) in 1923. But what is known is that the five main Scottish companies, of which the Highland was one, did not wish to amalgamate to form a separate independent Scottish Group, it being felt at the time that to amalgamate all of them into one consolidated system north of the border would not be viable in economic terms. Arising from this decision, the Caledonian (CR) and

Above: Elgin was the first place on the Inverness to Keith main line where the GNSR connected with the Highland line. Built by the original Inverness and Aberdeen Junction Railway, later a founding component of the HR, Elgin was given an attractive station, restrained in style but with ample facilities. It was the nearest point to Inverness reached by LNER locomotives and was well served by both companies. This undated LMS period view (c.1935?) shows platforms 5 and 6, the board in front of the smaller building nearest the camera reading "To LNER trains and Refreshment rooms" (Author's collection)

Below: Forres was the key location on the Inverness to Keith main line and enjoyed very good station facilities. Here, the line to Aviemore via Dava diverged from that to Elgin and beyond and a further line behind the buildings completed the triangle. This LMS view, undated but probably c.1930, shows the approach from the Inverness direction - the Aviemore line being on the right. Note the presence of almost brand new LMS standard carriage stock in the sidings and the still predominantly ash ballast. In later years, as part of its continued improvements to the line, mainly so as to accept larger and heavier engines compared with HR days, the LMS would replace all of this with more substantial track. (Author's collection)

This view, taken in 1928, shows the remote and barren nature of the mountain crossing at Druimuachdar summit on the Perth-Aviemore line. The picture is from the LMS period but the subject itself is pure Highland: Jones 'Goods' 4-6-0 No.17924 in charge of a northbound 'through freight', composed of loose-coupled wagons, almost all open types and very few with cargo protected by tarpaulin covers.

(The late H.C.Casserley)

Glasgow and South Western (G&SWR) systems fell naturally into the proposed LMS fold, given their pre-1923 associations with their English partners, the London and North Western (LNWR) and Midland (MR). In much the same way, the North British Railway (NBR) and GNSR were logical constituents of the LNER on the other side of the country.

But the Highland was different. It accepted through traffic at Perth from both sides of the country and worked it north therefrom in a wholly 'without prejudice' manner as far as can be judged. It could arguably and quite reasonably have been assigned to either of the two post-1922 companies operating in Scotland as far as its basic geography was concerned - it was dominantly an East Coast operation, after all. But as already mentioned, its main route north diverged directly from the Caledonian at Stanley Junction (to which place it had running powers over CR metals from Perth) and this is likely to have been a major contributory factor to the final decision. A further reason may have stemmed from the fact that the West Coast (LNWR/CR) and Midland contributions to through traffic for the Highland (both of them were in the LMS group, the latter

via the NBR from Carlisle and Edinburgh), were rather larger when combined than that which emanated from the pure East Coast Route equivalent, who knows? The distinctive pre-group railway geography of Scotland was to ensure that the Highland was not the only instance where the LMS and LNER 'changed sides' north of the border, of course, but it is as a constituent of the LMS that its later history must be appraised.

After a few years of settling down, the LMS, under the very celebrated Sir Josiah Stamp, later Lord Stamp of Shortlands, soon became an operation wherein the continuous reduction of operating costs (and all that pertained thereto) was dominant in its philosophy. This had wide ramifications across the whole spectrum of its activities, not least in the field of locomotive matters, perhaps the most obvious aspect to the majority of enthusiasts. Here, many economies could be achieved by way of standardisation across the board and the Highland part was not excluded from this appraisal, so we shall come back to it in due course. But this was not the whole story as far as the more distant parts of the LMS system were concerned.

There would be no point in achieving better operating costs in terms of locomotive matters if the traffic itself could not be sustained and this is where the LMS seems to have devoted a fair degree of initial emphasis. As far as freight traffic was concerned, after World War I and for many years thereafter representing some two thirds of total company revenue, things did not change too rapidly in the Highlands during the LMS period. Despite the increasing threat of road haulage elsewhere in Britain after WWI, the nature of the road infrastructure in the Highlands in those days ensured that freight traffic by rail remained fairly buoyant; and thus it was to prove for most of the LMS period and into early British Railways days too.

Sadly, in terms of future development, LMS freight trains were, for the most part, to retain the semi-archaic, loose-coupled and hand-braked nature which bedevilled the whole of Britain's railways far too long after 1923. Lack of effective long-distance road competition at the time, combined with the effect of often complacent railway management (manifested in its regular unwillingness to invest in more sophisticated goods vehicles), had not encouraged freight modernisation; and the road traffic and fuel restrictions of World War II were to ensure that this state of affairs continued well into the 1940s and 1950s. Thus it was that many elderly wagons were kept in service well beyond their 'sell-by' date as the only practical means of moving increasingly intensive wartime traffic, of which the Highland line bore more than a considerable share, not the least of which was the shifting of supplies to the far North to serve the Naval base at Scapa Flow. One result of this, beloved by enthusiasts and modellers alike, was the long retention in service of some of the more distinctive Highland vehicle types, not least its goods brake vans which were unlike those found anywhere else.

After the second world war, freight revenue slowly declined as the road alternative grew, but it was a gradual process for the most part and not until the A9 road from Perth to Inverness was progressively and extensively upgraded at huge cost in the 1970s and 1980s did things really change significantly, after which most rail-borne freight all but vanished. This situation is outwith our main concern, of course, but reverting to the post-1922 state of affairs, passenger demands began to change from a far earlier date and this *is* relevant to our story.

Here, the new-fangled motor car (which, at the time, did not demand quite such extensive road improvements as did commercial long-distance road haulage) was becoming a very real threat after WWI, albeit only available to wealthier folk at the time. Previously, it was these people who had patronised the HR by way of sending their carriage trucks, horseboxes and private saloons to the north of Perth in pursuit of their activities and it was a fine revenue earner for all concerned. But after the grouping, this traffic was in terminal decline, for it was these very same folk who could first afford to espouse the motor car.

A good friend of mine recounts the story of how one of his grandfathers sent his chauffeur north with the Daimler while the family took the sleeping car alternative. In somewhat

---

The commercial importance of the Far North line in LMS days is well exemplified by this busy view of Wick goods yard in 1939. Small consignment traffic clearly predominates and the number of covered vans (so as to protect the contents) is larger than would normally be expected on most goods trains of the time. The role of the horse in terms of local freight collection is also apparent and what is perhaps most surprising, given the obvious level of activity, is that there were serious proposals to shut the whole Highland Section down only a few years before this picture was taken. (Peter Tatlow Collection)

6

similar vein, the LMS cashed in on the motor car in a small way by providing a mini motorail service between Strathcarron and Kyle of Lochalsh during the 1930s (see also Chapter 3, Table III), thereby eliminating the need to negotiate what was not much more than an improved farm track further west for those wishing to take road vehicles to the Isle of Skye via the ferry crossing from Kyle of Lochalsh to Kyleakin. This road was not improved until well into the modern era as the writer can verify from his own experience during the 1960s and 1970s prior to considerable changes being made (including several stretches of completely new road) from Strathcarron to The Kyle itself.

However, countervening the decline in what might be called the 'horse and carriage trade' was the possibility of attracting a new sort of customer in the form of the growing middle classes who, although not yet always capable of moving into the fully motorised era, could still take advantage of their improved status by way of affording longer holidays. For them, a better type of carriage would be most acceptable.

Likewise, those many folk who relied on the railway simply to get them to work and/or visit such places as Perth, Glasgow, Dundee and Edinburgh in pursuit of business activities would

The direct Aviemore to Inverness line via Slochd Summit involved heavier civil engineering than previously seen on the Highland lines (see Chapter 2), well exemplified in this view of LMS standard Class 5P4F 2-6-0 No.13105 at Slochd Viaduct on 20th July 1931 with the 4.35pm Inverness-Perth train, typical of post-group practice on the line. At the head are LNER carriages for Kings's Cross (including sleeping cars of both classes), followed by an ex-MR twelve wheel clerestory dining car (transferred to the Highland by the LMS) and LMS sleeping cars (again both classes) for Euston. Perhaps the most difficult decision for Inverness passengers bound for London was to decide which of the options to take. (The late H.C.Casserley)

be more likely to use the railway if facilities were improved. This should not imply that the Highland was in any way a sort of commuter system in want of improvement - the very idea is absurd given its geography - nor was it an organisation which had neglected the needs of local passengers. In general, and even though the HR had (officially) phased out six-wheelers on its main lines before WWI, the fact remains that by 1923,

7

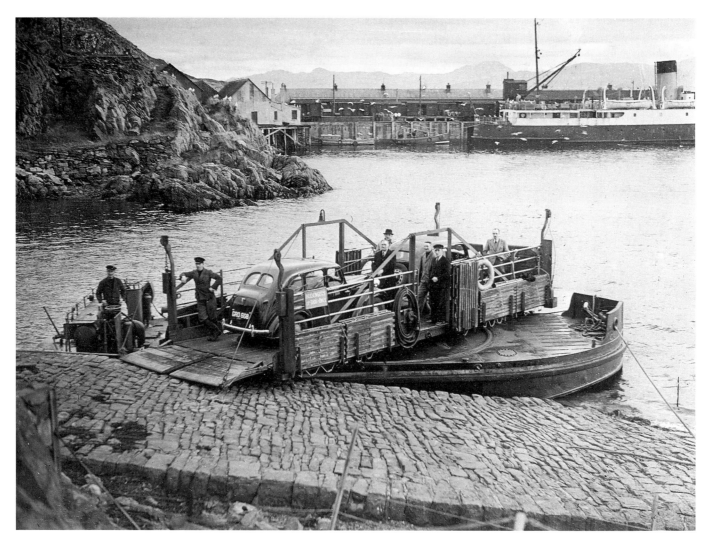

its carriage stock had, with a few exceptions, fallen behind that of most of the rest of Britain in terms of passenger expectation: something needed to be done and it was down to the LMS to address the problem.

In part this situation arose from the fact that the Highland had (perhaps prudently!) tended to assume that those many railways with which it was in contact - and whose carriages regularly ventured north of Perth - could be relied upon to provide something suitable for the longer-distance traveller. That we shall never know for sure, save to remark that the bulk of Highland carriages, albeit mounted on bogies, remained of non-corridor type, many without lavatories, and even the best of the Highland corridor types (very few in number but rather agreeable none the less) were usually confined to through services originating on the Highland system and were rarely, if ever, seen south of Edinburgh or Glasgow.

This was the situation which the LMS inherited in 1923 and it soon began to address the problem. Very soon after the Grouping, therefore, there began to be seen very many 'new' carriages on the Highland lines which were far better in terms of passenger amenity than those hitherto offered. They were often 'cascaded' types from other parts of the newly enlarged LMS system and regularly of some age in consequence. But

This fascinating LMS official view is back-stamped 1947, though it could perhaps have been taken a decade or so before, but not too much earlier judging by the style of motor cars. Whatever, it shows the Kyle-Kyleakin ferry at Kyle of Lochalsh jetty during final LMS days. The terminus of the line itself is in the background, partly hidden by the inevitable steamer and the picture truly encapsulates the very different nature of the Highland in LMS days..... (Author's collection)

they were none the worse for that and allowed many older HR 'boneshakers', usually six-wheel types, to be scrapped.

Likewise, on more prestigious turns, it was not long after 1922 before the LMS began to insert both corridor and dining cars into the reckoning to a far greater extent than hitherto. For the most part, these too were mainly 'hand me downs' from the other parts of the system as new standard LMS types began to appear on its principal services elsewhere. But such 'cascaded' types were always of good quality (some of them were actually fairly new and lasted in service well into post-LMS days) and served to show that the LMS, albeit mindful of the 'pennies' throughout its whole existence, was not in the business of

This mid-1920s view at Elgin shows an unidentified local train heading towards Keith behind 'Small Ben' 4-4-0 No.14400 Ben More. It is wholly typical of the early LMS period in that the locomotive now has a Caledonian type boiler, the main carriage in the train is an early LMS standard non-corridor composite and the trailing six-wheel third class is probably ex-Midland (details unclear). The LMS carriage on its own (larger than previous HR types) could carry 72T + 24F, probably enough for normal needs, so the presumption must be that the trailing six-wheeler was a strengthener. Meantime, the ex-HR bogie full brake hints at a large amount of parcels trade and appears still to be in green livery. (Author's collection)

closing down services if it could, by selective improvement of facilities at modest cost, keep them going.

Thus it was that the Highland was a major beneficiary of this sort of new thinking and it is by no means unreasonable to postulate that this was a major factor in terms of the longer term survival of the vast bulk of its whole system; and in this lies much of the post-1922 interest. Whatever the reasons, the fact is that the Highland Section (as it was now called), soon became the recipient of a wide variety of 'new' carriage types which remained for many a long year and thus served to keep most services reasonably viable during a difficult time. That they also inserted a veritable cornucopia of carriage styles into the scene for the delectation of enthusiasts came by way of a total bonus: they undoubtedly added considerable interest.....

Changes were not confined to carriage types, however. The matter of locomotive provisioning also received attention and here, it is difficult to isolate the Highland lines from the overall LMS locomotive policy throughout its Northern Division, as the LMS system in Scotland was known at the time. The key word was 'standardisation', something of a company 'mantra' throughout its existence as far as the LMS was concerned, the general philosophy being that significant cost savings could be achieved with fewer and more modern classes of locomotives, built in quantity, rather than continue with the huge inherited variety of types, many of them very few in absolute numbers and often obsolescent if not obsolete.

The most obvious form of locomotive standardisation was to be seen in the form of new standard types put into service as a result of the familiar LMS 'Scrap and Build' policy, be it under the initial Hughes/Fowler/Lemon locomotive régimes of 1923-31 or the later Stanier period from 1932 onwards. The implementation of this policy, company-wide, would take time to complete, of course, and it is a matter of history that the LMS did not last long enough for this to happen in full, though it did come quite close. Meantime, the traffic still had to be handled and in this context, the LMS Northern Division took on a very distinctive character, largely in consequence of the locomotive evolution of its three Scottish constituents.

By far the biggest of these was the Caledonian, which had, prior to 1923, already embarked upon a very high degree of locomotive standardisation along lines first set out by that most celebrated engineer Dugald Drummond, who was followed in due course and virtually seamless fashion by a very fine series of locomotive chiefs (Lambie, McIntosh and Pickersgill), all of whom were to develop Drummond's essential principles in progressively enlarged form, with but few and insignificant exceptions, until the end of the CR period. Curiously enough, this long continuum, often referred to as the 'Scottish School' of locomotive design, actually started on the Highland Railway itself during the later 1860s under William Stroudley, for whom Drummond worked for many years both on the HR and on the London, Brighton and South Coast Railway, to which both of them moved in 1869.

Drummond came back to Scotland as the NBR locomotive chief in 1875 and moved to the Caledonian in 1882, whereafter he began to institute a locomotive progression which served the Caledonian well for the rest of its life. The CR thus entered

the LMS with a fleet of robust and mostly trouble-free designs which had been built in some quantity and mostly to relatively few wheel arrangements, of which 4-4-0s, 0-6-0s and 0-4-4Ts dominated. Unsurprisingly, therefore, the LMS, as an interim move until new standard types began to appear, resolved on a quasi-standardisation in its Northern Division, largely based on former Caledonian precepts. It made much sense.

The consequences were interesting to say the least. Against this scenario, the G&SWR locomotive fleet, less than half the size of the CR contribution, but which did include some quite interesting types, mostly reflected a wholly different design philosophy, incompatible with CR practice. Its locomotives were a swift casualty in consequence, most of them simply

---

Gollanfield Junction was the point where the Fort George Branch joined the Inverness-Keith main line. This view, taken looking towards Inverness, cannot be earlier than 1929-30, the time when the LMS carriage (a corridor brake composite) seen in the right hand (branch) platform was built, nor can it be much later than 1934 when the LMS began to remove the side lights above the guard's lookout - near end of the carriage. But it clearly indicates the speed at which the LMS introduced its latest carriage types onto even the humblest services, this one being one of the earliest examples where the draughty outside doors to compartments were suppressed. (Author's collection)

Scottish Locomotive School - Jones Highland style: In the first view, one of many inherited 'Crewe Type' 4-4-0s and the sole surviving 'Bruce' Class 4-4-0 - LMS 14278 - is seen starting to run round its train at Fochabers on 16th May 1928. Apart from replacement Drummond chimney, all else is pure David Jones.

Many would aver that Jones' 'Loch' Class 4-4-0s were the aesthetic high point of this celebrated designer's work. This is LMS No.14395, Loch Garve, resplendent in pre-1928 crimson livery at Kyle of Lochalsh in the mid-1920s and still carrying the original Jones louvred chimney. In later LMS times, the 'Lochs' would receive Caledonian type boilers and lose their distinctive chimneys, but their outside cylinders and Stroudley-style cab roofs always gave them a bit of an artistic edge... (Author's collection; Peter Tatlow Collection)

serving out their time until heavy repairs were due (mainly when their boilers wore out) and then being scrapped.

But the Highland locomotive fleet, albeit numerically small compared with even the modest G&SWR totals, fared better than the latter. This was because most Highland designs were also firmly grounded in the Scottish School, this time via such well known engineers as David Jones (works manager to the aforementioned William Stroudley on the HR before taking over after Stroudley moved south) and Peter Drummond, who was Dugald's younger brother and much influenced by him. As a result, the Jones 'Loch' Class 4-4-0s and many later Peter Drummond HR types could accept Caledonian type boilers and fittings when major repairs were due, thus permitting their post-1922 lives to be considerably extended.

The upshot was that in Scotland, relatively few of the newer LMS standard designs played too much part on ex-HR lines until well into the 1930s. This was in marked contrast to the ex-G&SWR system where, from the mid-1920s, new standard LMS types of largely Midland inspiration (mainly 4-4-0s and 0-6-0s) soon saw off the bulk of the old G&SWR fleet.

There were exceptions, of course, which Chapter 5 will consider in more detail, notably but not exclusively the later and fairly widespread importation of ex-CR designs onto the Highland routes. However, since these types were visually very similar to many of the native HR designs, it is probably not too sweeping a generalisation to say that the Highland Section retained more of its original pre-1923 characteristics in terms of locomotive lineaments than did most parts of the LMS until at least the mid-1930s and beyond. This 'distinctive difference', if thus we may describe it, may well be a further reason why the Highland was always popular amongst railway enthusiasts, especially when taken with the variety of coaching stock which was to be seen in consequence of the 'cascading' policy outlined above.

And one thing which changed hardly at all was the basic infrastructure itself. This aspect of the post-1922 railway scene in Britain was not confined to Highland lines, of course, for most companies had built their permanent structures (stations, goods sheds &c) to last. Where not closed down fully in later years, many places have retained their original structures to this day in all parts of the country, largely unchanged from pre-group times, save for some modernisation of facilities, a bit of simplification and the rationalisation of many track layouts. The Highland was no different from the norm and its major stations were often rather impressive.

Unlike some companies, however, the HR did not employ a specific 'house style' in its architecture, save perhaps for some smaller stations where passenger facilities were often very spartan and utilitarian in nature, receiving basic standard structures in consequence, which were regularly likened to 'tin tabernacles' because of their corrugated iron roofs. But for a company which was never the richest of concerns, it did at least offer these basic facilities in some very remote areas and gained respect for so doing - and the LMS did its best to retain this commendable feature for as long as possible. Additionally, the Highland had its own characteristic lineside features, amongst which might perhaps be mentioned its distinctively styled signals and their associated signal cabins which were remarkably consistent throughout the system and lasted for many a long year, often into post-LMS days.

What is also, perhaps, worthy of note at this stage is that with one minor exception (the link between Keith and Buckie at the interface with the GNSR), the whole of the Highland's route network was to pass intact to the LMS. Even afterwards, the LMS was to initiate very few additional line closures, a fact which Chapter 4 will try to amplify. In effect, the LMS made almost no real changes to the essential nature of the Highland system during its period in charge. Such changes as it made were gradual and modest, largely by way of renewing worn-out parts, rather than dramatic and draconian, though there were, eventually, many of them. In fact, as later chapters will try to reveal, the LMS not only retained most of the route system itself, but also made very considerable attempts to retain and in many cases improve the facilities it inherited. These were still the days when service mattered, even to a hard-nosed commercial operation like the LMS.

Other than locomotive and rolling stock changes, outlined above but which will be considered in more detail later, the most obvious difference after 1922 was the adoption of new locomotive and carriage liveries, whose rather more decorative and Midland-derived style, compared with the plain green of the HR in its final pre-group years, seems to have been embraced with considerable enthusiasm by those charged with making such changes, not least at the ex-HR Lochgorm works. Here, it is perhaps worth remarking that although this place was to retain an active repair capacity until well into BR days, it became increasingly common for the larger HR locomotives (especially those which could accept CR type fittings - above) to be sent to St Rollox (ex-CR) or even Kilmarnock works (ex-G&SWR) for their major overhauls.

All of which said, it nevertheless remains largely true that, cosmetics and (some) rolling stock changes apart, the Highland lines north of Perth retained most of their essential pre-1923 ambience throughout the LMS period, certainly until the start of the second world war and for a few years thereafter. Indeed, it was only in BR days that really fundamental *conceptual* changes began - the lines north of Perth being, for example, one of the first parts of the whole BR system to be completely dieselised, the cost of hauling locomotive coal having become rather costly, much as it did in Cornwall too - another region at the extremity of the British system. But this is well outside our period, so the remainder of these pages will concentrate on showing something of how the LMS itself went about ensuring the long-term survival of one of the most interesting parts of its disparate inheritance.

LMS

Scottish Locomotive School - Peter Drummond Highland style: The Drummond 'Castle' Class 4-6-0s of 1900 were an interesting combination of the David Jones' outside cylinder style (as seen on his Goods 4-6-0s of 1894) with Drummond's own later ideas. The result was a very handsome design, repeated in some quantity by Highland standards and lasting until the very end of the LMS period - see Chapter 5. Here, LMS No.14688 Thurso Castle is seen entering Aviemore in June 1927. Apart from the locomotive itself, the carriages are a fascinating assemblage and wholly typical of the 1920s LMS scene - see Chapter 3. Back from the tender, the first six, all corridor types, can positively be identified: ex-LNWR; ex-HR; ex-CR; ex-NBR; ex-LNWR; ex-WCJS, the latter

being a twelve-wheel composite dining car transferred to the Highland Section after the grouping by the LMS.

The rather imposing 0-6-4Ts of 1909 were the last Peter Drummond design for the Highland, after which he went to the G&SWR and continued in much the same visual vein. The big tank engines were typically 'Drummond' in outline and mostly confined to banking duties from Blair Atholl - the HR was not really known for using tank engines on the main line. This view is therefore somewhat different in showing the first of the class (LMS No.15300) on local freight duty at Elgin in August 1925. Numbered in the LMS passenger series (15XXX) it carried red livery accordingly - see Chapter 5.

(The late H.C.Casserley; Peter Tatlow Collection)

A typical example of a Caledonian boiler fitted to an ex-Highland type: Perth-based LMS No.14384 Loch Laggan at Blair Atholl in the late 1930s with a southbound local train consisting of the familiar eclectic mixture of carriages. On this occasion an ex-LNWR 57ft third class non-corridor leads, then comes a short bogie non-corridor (?ex-G&SWR or MR?), with but six compartments, probably downgraded ex-first class. The next pair are bogie full brakes (ex-MR and, probably, ex-CR) which suggests a fair amount of parcels traffic (see Chapter 3), while the train is terminated by a much newer LMS standard 57ft non-corridor composite. (Author's collection)

At various intermediate places along the line outwith the obvious major traffic centres, the Highland located a few small engine sheds to serve its local needs, and the LMS continued in like manner for many years. There was nothing elaborate about them and this is a typical example: the simple but adequate facility provided at Helmsdale with 4-4-0 No.14410 Ben Dearg in residence in the 1920s. (Author's collection)

One of the ironies of the final 25 years of private operation of our railways before 1948 was that 'service' was often regarded as rather more important by these so-called hard nosed commercial operations than many latter-day folk, who can see nothing good in the pre-1948 scene, are prepared to admit; but here is proof that they may just be mistaken. In the first view, taken at Golspie on the Far North line in July 1931, there is no lack of patronage to be seen. In particular, it may be noted that the carriage nearest to the bridge is a dining car, ex-Lancashire and Yorkshire Railway as it so happens but not really important in context. How many places of this size are thus served in our modern era?

Even more extraordinary is the second picture which shows what was known as a 'ladder stop' between Achnashellach and Achnasheen on the Kyle line. The date and service is unknown but is certainly of LMS vintage and clearly shows that the train could and would (in extremis) stop anywhere to serve the public. And lest some folk should think that this is impossible to achieve in modern circumstances, the last time the author witnessed anything of like kind was as recently as 1997 when no less than the prestigious Via Rail Trans-Canada 'Canadian' express (on which he was riding) was flagged down to pick up just a couple of folk from the lineside in the remote fastnesses of Ontario.   (The late H.C.Casserley; the late Gavin Wilson)

The Highland Section adopted the new LMS liveries with enthusiasm, wasting no time in giving the elaborately lined LMS crimson to any type which qualified for such treatment. It is hard to know why this should have been the case, for old allegiances died hard after the grouping and there were many instances where the new styles were not too well received. Maybe in the Highland Section, the pre-group unlined green was felt to be a bit boring and the painters welcomed more of a challenge to their skills. That we shall never know, but the fact is that the Highland fleet was one of the quickest to assume the new style and it is hard to pick but

one exemplar, given that for some strange and inexplicable reason, 'Midland Lake' seemed to suit most of those to which it was applied.

The first picture shows the unique Jones 0-4-4T No.15050 in the pre-1928 red livery c.1928, at which time it was used on the Wick and Lybster branch until withdrawal in 1929. In the second view, taken after the LMS altered its livery, insignia style and positioning in 1928, Cumming 'Clan Goods' 4-6-0 No.17951 is seen in an immaculately presented version of the lined black livery officially

allocated to mixed traffic and secondary passenger types after 1927 but not strictly applicable to goods engines. Lochgorm seems to have ignored this diktat and turned out quite a few goods types in lined black livery for a few years. There is some evidence that this lining was yellow rather than the official vermilion, but confirmation is lacking. Purely for the record, the designation 'Clan Goods' was unofficial. The engines preceded the 'Clans' into service and only after the latter had appeared did the goods version begin to be referred to in the popular form used throughout this book. (Author's collection - 2)

2

Geography and Infrastructure

THE HIGHLAND NETWORK at its maximum extent formed a classic example of the way in which the growth of railways was affected by the underlying realities of both economics and geography wherein, first and foremost, it is vital to have a sound commercial reason for any line of railway. Only when the full economic rationale of any proposal is taken into account can the nature of the underlying geography begin to assert influence and this was certainly true of the Highland and accounts in large part both for the nature of its evolution as a system and its later outward and visible form. However, before considering this matter in detail, a few preliminary comments are felt to be appropriate.

The rapid growth of railways during mid-Victorian times was as much due to the lack of any suitable alternative as to anything else, for this was a time of economic expansion when to be denied access to modern transport was, in effect, to condemn the region in question to a slow and inexorable decline. That much has not changed, of course, save that we now have a number of alternative choices, thanks to road and air, both of which have found their place in the Scottish Highlands. But like so many other parts of Great Britain, had it not been for the railway in the first place, there may well have been no significant economic activity left on which the newer forms of transport could build.

The fundamental problem with a railway is, of course, its need to keep to a near-level alignment as far as possible, preferably avoiding too many sharp curves. Ideally, this should run hand-in-hand with the minimum of heavy civil engineering as well, for this only added to the building costs; but it is not quite as simple as that. For example, it is often presumed that railways tend to keep to valleys so as to avoid steep gradients and keep costs down, whereas roads are not so restricted and can go more or less anywhere within reason. As a broad form of generalisation this contains an element of historical truth, but if the economic imperative did not exist in the first place, even the best of valleys would not, taken simply on its own, attract a railway. Conversely, if there was good economic reason for connecting two places separated by less favourable territory, then a railway might well be attempted despite any difficulties posed by the terrain.

In the very early days, it was often supposed that railways could not cope with steeper grades at all, so the cost of heavy engineering in order to maintain a near-level alignment was often accepted if the traffic potential was high, the London and Birmingham Railway of 1838 being a wholly typical example of this way of thinking. Once it had surmounted the initial steep 1:70 climb out of Euston to Camden to clear the Regent's Canal (the bank was worked by rope haulage until locomotives could cope with the gradient), the steepest grade was never more than 1:320 and resulted in some of the finest railway civil engineering then or subsequently - most of it still in use.

The only practical alternative to heavy engineering in those early days was to accept much more circuitous routes in order to keep the line reasonably level. This often led to much cost saving in constructional terms, even if the line did not take the most direct route, and became a popular choice in many cases where underlying economics did not justify the heavier costs of building a speedier and shorter option. In this respect, the construction of early railways tempts close comparison with that of the inland waterways a generation or two earlier.

It was not long, however, before it was realised that steam locomotives could cope with far steeper gradients than had at first been thought and by the later 1840s, many lines were being built whose gradients would have been unheard of in the pioneering days. This added complication to the fairly simple 'choice of two options' outlined above and it was well into this later phase that the first elements of what was soon to become the Highland Railway came onto the scene. By then, steeper gradients could be accepted and if, by adopting them, a shorter line could be constructed, so much the better.

Yet again, this is not quite as simple as it seems, for this sort of approach could not be divorced from construction costs in areas such as the Highlands where the economic rationale often bordered on the marginal. In consequence, the evolution of its network tended to be a conservative business where the underlying geography was more often than not the determining factor until greater traffic potential allowed the expense of shortening distances by more extravagant civil engineering to be contemplated. Thus it was that since steeper gradients could be surmounted from the time the very first line was built out of Inverness, their main use in many cases was simply to reduce construction costs by allowing the line to adopt a much more switchback profile rather than lessen the gradients by way of increasing the amount of civil engineering, or even using them to shorten the journey itself for that matter. So let us see how the Highland system evolved against this scenario, this time dealing with the lines in the order in which they were built.

Orton station in June 1937, looking towards Inverness. At this point, the Inverness to Keith line descended for a mile or so at 1:100 (right of camera) before tackling some 2.5 uphill miles at 1:60 towards Mulben, by far the steepest gradient on what became the Highland Railway (after the early 1860s amalgamations) until the direct line to the south via Slochd summit was completed. The station is restrained but substantial and there is little hint of the demanding terrain which the line met between the Spey Valley and Keith.

(Author's collection)

Orbliston Junction was where the Fochabers branch linked with the Inverness to Keith main line - see also Chapter 4. This May 1930 view shows the Fochabers branch train in the bay with Jones 'Strath' Class 4-4-0 (LMS No.14274 Strathcarron) in charge. The train itself consists of a single ex-HR lavatory non-corridor (probably 1st/3rd composite) and a six-wheel ex-Midland full brake transferred to the Highland area soon after 1922. The featureless background exemplifies the predominantly easy terrain over which the Inverness-Keith line was built - see text.

(The late H.C.Casserley)

Elgin looking east, probably during the 1930s. Straight ahead is the Highland main line to Keith, while diverging to the left is the GNSR coastal route to Portessie which, soon after diverging from the HR, led to a further junction which was the start of the GNSR's own more circuitous route to Keith (see map on rear cover). An unidentified Highland 'Small Ben' 4-4-0 is in the left foreground with a Keith train and a former GNSR 4-4-0 waits in the spur beyond the water tower.

(Author's collection)

Inverness to Keith

The first line to be opened throughout, that to Elgin and Keith, had a relatively easy time of it for the most part in terms of gradients and engineering, as did the bulk of its continuation to Aberdeen via the GNSR for that matter - no doubt a reason why they were first on the scene. Built along the coastal plain from Inverness, it follows an undulating and presumably fairly cheap to build route with little to cause concern until reaching Elgin, save for a short pitch of about two miles at 1:103 between Kinloss and Alves. Even after Elgin, after which the terrain becomes a litle more demanding, there was little of major consequence save for a steep climb at 1:60 for just over two miles between Orton and Mulben as the line passes out of the Spey valley. It is presumed that the cost of reducing this gradient by way of more dramatic civil engineering was felt to be too expensive in view of its short nature.

For the most part, the Inverness-Keith line represents the classic early form of railway construction - ie a low level route across easy territory which, fortuitously in the circumstances, also happened to be the most nearly direct. It uses the coast plain and smaller valleys almost throughout its length, the only concession to its role as part of a longer route to Aberdeen as far as the Highland was concerned being where it follows a shorter and more steeply graded alignment between Elgin and Orton via Orbliston (just over three miles mostly at 1:98) rather than continue east over slightly easier country to reach the Tay near Fochabers and then turn south following the Tay valley proper. The by-passing of Fochabers in this way had some interesting consequences in the branch line context as will be seen in Chapter 4.

Stanley Junction in LMS days - date unspecified but after replacement LMS upper quadrant signal arms had started to take over from earlier types. This was the true start of the Highland main line to Inverness - Caledonian double track main line to Aberdeen straight ahead, Highland line diverging left - and was worked in a distinctive manner. Northbound trains for the HR route used the right hand line at the island platform, taking the single line tablet at the divergence from the CR line below the footbridge, but southbound trains were worked into the left hand side of the island platform (ie 'wrong road') so as to keep them clear of the Caledonian main line until a path was clear, the set of the points in the foreground suggesting that a southbound working from the Highland line was probably due. (The late H.C.Casserley)

Perth to Inverness

Turning now to the direct routes north from Perth, these lines are the first and only major examples on the Highland where the economic need to shorten the journey began to take some degree of precedence over geographical difficulties, albeit not entirely so in the case of the earlier route via Forres once the line had reached Aviemore from the south. But regardless of which route was chosen north of Aviemore, its alignment to that place from Stanley Junction was wholly pre-determined by the underlying physical geography, there being really only one possibility available, even though not exactly 'as the crow flies' when seen on the map. That the modern A9 trunk road follows exactly the same route is no coincidence.....

The Pass of Killiecrankie is so narrow that the only way the railway could negotiate the restricted entrance to the valley was by means of a ten-arch viaduct, immediately followed by a short tunnel. This undated early picture shows the structure rather more clearly than do later views, taken after tree growth had filled much of the surrounding area. The view is upstream, the line from Perth entering from the right.

(Author's collection)

On leaving Stanley, and after making full use of the mostly undemanding territory across the Vale of Strathmore to reach Dunkeld, the line first takes advantage of many available valleys through the Grampians formed by the River Tay and its tributaries. The Tay itself is followed to Ballinluig, whence the Aberfeldy branch (see Chapter 4) continues to make further progress along that river, leaving the main line to follow the River Tummel for a short distance through Pitlochry. The Tummel valley serves for a few miles only because, like the Tay, its alignment then takes a due westerly direction, the main line being now obliged to continue northwards via the rather more difficult narrow entrance to the valley of the River Garry at the famous pass of Killiecrankie.

From here, Glen Garry is followed via Blair Atholl to the watershed at Druimuachdar summit, close by those evocatively named twin peaks, the Sow of Atholl and Boar of Badenoch.

At this point, the line then follows the northward flowing valleys of the rivers Truim and Spey, the latter being joined a mile or so south of Newtonmore, whence the line has an easy and gently undulating passage to Aviemore itself.

Although the ascents in either direction to Druimuachdar from Blair Atholl and Newtonmore were tough (the former is longer and more demanding with steepest gradients at 1:70), and presented a formidable task to locomotives, especially in steam days, the route to Aviemore from Dunkeld is essentially a traditional 'valley floor concept' from start to finish. This enables it to manage with relatively few major engineering works and a noteworthy absence of long tunnels, there being but three very short and unavoidable examples of the latter - the only tunnels on the Highland at all for that matter. Perhaps the most spectacular structure is the well known viaduct at Killiecrankie, closely followed by the girder bridge near

The bleak mountain crossing at Dalnaspidal, a mile or two short of Druimuachdar summit itself. The view is looking west along Loch Garry and the locomotive is 4-4-0 No.14393 Loch Laoghal, *probably involved in piloting or banking duty. Though the date is mid-May 1928, a storm sheet is still rigged between engine and tender which suggests a fair amount of tender first running.*
(The late H.C.Casserley)

Aviemore, the principal traffic centre between Perth and Inverness, was given comprehensive facilities. These two early official views (undated but probably just pre-LMS) show the station much as it was at the end of Highland days. The view south shows the substantial and attractive buildings provided on both main platforms, while the view north hints at some of the signalling complexity at the divergence of the two routes north. The junction itself was to the left of the locomotive depot seen in the far right distance. (Author's collection - 2)

Boat of Garten was another junction between the GNSR and Highland systems, the former taking the Spey valley north to Keith and Elgin. This undated but LMS period view shows the LMS line (left) and LNER route (right), the actual point of junction being near to the signal cabin. Both lines followed near-parallel routes down this part of the Spey for most of the way to Grantown and the picture clearly shows the generally easy nature of the terrain - see text.
(The late Gavin Wilson)

Boat of Garten station itself in June 1937 - a typical Highland mixture of stone and pre-fabricated buildings. The LNER mostly used the right hand platform, seen here occupied by pre-group stock from that company. Looking through the typical lattice footbridge into the distance (beyond the signal cabin near the double signal posts), what looks rather like an approaching ex-GNSR 4-4-0 can just be distinguished on the original print.
(The late Gavin Wilson Collection)

Dalguise; but given the c.77 mile length of the route between Stanley and Aviemore, it is quite remarkable that such rugged terrain could be overcome with a maximum gradient of 1:70 at such modest expense in terms of civil engineering.

North of Aviemore, however, things were different and the fact that two routes were eventually provided provides an interesting reflection on the gradual evolution of the economic side of the railway building equation. The problem here lies in the 'grain' of the landscape north of Aviemore, whose ridges and valleys are mostly aligned SW-NE - ie at right angles to the preferred short cut to Inverness. The simple option would have been to follow the easier low level Spey valley route via Craigellachie and Rothes-on-Spey to Elgin. But this somewhat extended diversion would have lost much of the advantage of the new shorter route to Aviemore, not to mention getting close to GNSR territory; and it is unlikely that the Highland would want *that* company involved given their rivalry at the time. Accordingly, the chosen route via Forres was, in effect, a sort of compromise, probably motivated by the fact that having considerably shortened the distance to Aviemore already, some degree of additional expense - ie avoiding some but not all parts of the major obstacle, but tackling the latter where the shortening of distance made sense - was justifiable.

This line therefore follows the relatively easy Spey valley route only as far as Grantown-on-Spey at which point it was possible to use minor tributaries of the Spey and Findhorn rivers to get across the physical divide at Dava Moor, thence joining the Findhorn valley proper to reach Forres. The ascents to Dava from either side were assymetric. That from Grantown was the shorter (some six miles) and mostly at 1:80, whereas it was a very long flog of some eighteen miles from Forres to the summit, mostly at 1:70-75 with a slight easing near Dunphail, near which was the only other major structure on the original

The almost featureless Dava moor with a southbound sleeping car train of mixed LMS and LNER stock for Euston and King's Cross headed by 'Large Ben' 4-4-0 No.14419 Ben Mholach. This train would probably amalgamate at Aviemore with further carriages via the Slochd summit route. Note that for both companies, a brake composite is accompanied by a first class sleeping car and the lack of third class sleeping cars suggests a pre-1928 date. The last coach with its recessed entrances cannot be identified, but could be a special saloon of some kind.

(The late Gavin Wilson Collection)

route between Perth and Inverness: a seven arch viaduct across the Divie river. In locomotive terms the ascents to Dava were almost as tough as those to Druimuachdar further south; but they were certainly no worse.

The whole route was opened in 1863 and it was not until a generation later that further agitation for an even shorter route between Aviemore and Inverness began to be investigated, in part prompted by threats of a rival route up the Great Glen from the south to Inverness, supported *inter alia* by the North British Railway. The Highland took it seriously and, despite the prospect of little if any extra revenue, the final short cut to Inverness from Aviemore via Carr Bridge and Slochd summit took shape over a long gestation period from 1884 until its opening by stages between 1892 and 1898.

By this time, politics certainly outweighed geography and the new line employed exceptionally heavy engineering works, including two memorable viaducts over the Findhorn and Nairn rivers at Tomatin and Culloden respectively. The only modest concession to geography, in reality unavoidable given the lie of the land, was the climb out of Inverness where the

Carr Bridge station in 1931, looking north on the direct line via Slochd. The start of the 1:60 can clearly be seen in the distance, and beyond it, the nature of the hills which this line traverses can be appreciated.

(The late H.C.Casserley)

line makes an easterly detour to gain the Nairn valley near Culloden. This ascent, which starts only a mile or so out of Inverness, is mostly at 1:60/1:70, the physical geography of the area being almost wholly against the railway. This final route not only contains many miles of the steepest gradients to be found anywhere between Inverness and Perth (1:60) but its summit at Slochd (1,315ft) is 263ft higher than Dava (1,052ft) and only 169ft below that of Druimuachdar (1,484ft). What is more, the vertical difference in level between Inverness and Slochd is well in excess of the two other major Highland banks (Blair Atholl to Druimuachdar and Forres to Dava). But yet again, by making what use it could of such minor tributary valleys as were on offer, the line avoided any tunnels.

Cumming 4-6-0s in the shape of No.17950 (leading) and No.14766 Clan Chattan *start off south from Inverness in August 1939 with a double-headed express freight via the direct line. Note that the 1:60 gradient has already started (see text) and a few hundred yards further on, the line swings right to cross over the main line to Forres and Keith seen in the left foreground. Note the ex-Caledonian 0-6-0T on the latter line - see also Chapter 5.*

(Peter Tatlow Collection)

24

Achterneed is some half way up the four mile 1:50 climb from Fodderty Junction to Raven's Rock. The gradient reduces to 1:350 through the station, the easing at the end of the first two miles being clearly seen beyond the platform. Until the building of the Strathpeffer branch, this station took the name of the spa town itself, almost two miles away down a steep hill. It will be noted that the facilities provided at this, the first station to serve Strathpeffer, are nothing like as elaborate as were later to be provided - see Chapter 4.

(The late Gavin Wilson Collection)

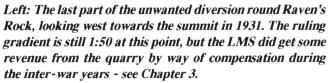

Left: The last part of the unwanted diversion round Raven's Rock, looking west towards the summit in 1931. The ruling gradient is still 1:50 at this point, but the LMS did get some revenue from the quarry by way of compensation during the inter-war years - see Chapter 3.

(The late Gavin Wilson Collection)

The Northern routes from Inverness

Although the lines to the Far North and the Kyle of Lochalsh mostly post-dated those to the south and east of Inverness, save for the Slochd Summit cut-off route (above), they were, taken together, fine examples of where the economics of the proposed line(s) were insufficiently robust to allow too many liberties to be taken with the underlying geography. Such form of generalisation is always dangerous, of course, but it seems fair to state that for the most part they took the easiest options possible in terms of route finding and, in consequence, tended

to adopt more circuitous alignments, mainly to reduce building costs. But this also allowed them to serve many small (but in context significant) settlements which tended to be located mostly in the valley bottoms or on the coastal fringes which might have been ignored by more direct routes.

They shared a route to Dingwall whose alignment made no attempt to shorten the distance from Inverness by bridging the Beauly Firth just north of the Highland capital - technically more than feasible but economically out of the question. At Dingwall, the line to The Kyle struck almost due west and this will be the first to be considered.

Perusal of the map suggests that this line might have been easier to achieve had it departed from the main line to Wick at Muir of Ord, whence it would have encountered rather simpler terrain via Contin as far as Loch Garve, conceivably even as far as Lochluichart had it taken the available Conon valley route from Contin. However, Dingwall was the most important town in this region and it no doubt made much economic sense to make this the junction point. Even so, full advantage was not taken when building the first part of the line.

The most logical route west of Dingwall was and still is via Strathpeffer and Contin, after which there was the choice of routes to Lochluichart (above). But the citizens of Strathpeffer steadfastly opposed the building of a railway in the initial days

25

Achnasheen marked the effective 'half way point' on the Skye line and was close by the summit at Luib. It was hardly a substantial settlement, most of its activity being centred on the railway itself, but it was on relatively low lying ground at the convergence of several valleys, thus becoming something of a gathering point for traffic. It was one of the two largest stations between Dingwall and The Kyle and, during quieter seasons, was also the point of transfer of dining cars between west- and eastbound trains.
(The late Gavin Wilson Collection)

Strathcarron, the second substantial station on the Skye route, was additionally significant during traditional railway times because, until quite recently (late 1960s/early 1970s), it marked the end of any sort of decent road further west. This official view, taken in 1939 at 1.00pm if the station clock is right, quite apart from giving a clear impression of a well-kept spacious station (a very common and commendable feature of the Highland lines), also shows the attempts made by the LMS to provide for motor traffic - see also Chapters 1 and 3. In the middle distance, three loaded open carriage trucks can be seen, probably about to unload, and one suspects that this may have been one reason why the picture was taken.
(LMS Official)

The approach to The Kyle was very difficult to achieve in purely engineering terms - no doubt why it was many years after reaching Strome Ferry before the line was finally extended. This undated view is indicative of just some of the problems, which did not change in any significant way until the abandonment of steam. On the right, the main line is seen approaching via a near vertical-sided cutting while on the left, further rock removal was necessary, not only to create level space, but also to give access to an all-essential turntable (far distance). From this approach line, access could then be gained to the locomotive shed itself (left).

(The late Gavin Wilson Collection)

(see also Chapter 4) and, in consequence, the Dingwall and Skye line was forced to deviate via Raven's Rock summit, thus causing a wholly unnecessary lengthening of the route and a severe 'blip' in the gradient profile (1:50). This had a further knock-on effect in the shape of another similar 'hump' between Garve and Lochluichart (Corriemuillie) which would not have been there if the Conon valley route (again see above) had been chosen, though Garve itself would have been by-passed and this may have been an important consideration.

From Lochluichart, the line is a typical valley bottom route entirely determined by geography, following Strathbran to just beyond Achnasheen at Luib Summit (646ft), thence via Glen Carron and the delectable south shore of Loch Carron to Kyle of Lochalsh itself. As it transpired, this route was also very direct, unlike the Far North equivalent, but this benefit was no more than fortuitous in the circumstances. The ruling gradient

is 1:50 but, apart from the Raven's Rock and Corriemuillie diversions (above), such instances are very short indeed and arise mostly because the line was laid on the surface, as far as technically possible, to save construction costs. As a result of this, the number of subtle gradient changes on the Kyle line (and the very short distances between them) is probably more than anywhere else on the Highland. In effect, the line climbs gently to Luib from Lochluichart, descends more steeply to just east of Achnashellach (at which point there is a slight 'hump') and thence more gently to Strathcarron.

The Far North line from Dingwall is not dissimilar in basic principle - ie seeking the easiest route - but it takes a far more circuitous course north of Tain. As far as that point, it follows a simple and undulating route along the easy coastal plain, but then takes on quite different characteristics by making a huge inward salient round the inner end of Dornoch Firth and thence to Lairg, rather than cross the firth at some convenient earlier point. As with the Beauly Firth (above) a shorter route which bridged the Dornoch Firth just north of Tain was technically possible, but was undoubtedly a case where ease of building outweighed the cost of a more direct route. Even so, between Invershin and Rogart, even this perambulating line has to climb eight miles or so (and descend therefrom) on gradients mostly between 1:70 and 1:80 before regaining the coast at The Mound (the junction for the Dornoch branch - Chapter 4).

North of The Mound, this part of the line (much of which was promoted by the 4th Duke of Sutherland who, along with his successors, had his own private station at Dunrobin during both Highland and LMS days) has an easy switchback route along the coastal fringe via Brora to Helmsdale, whence it again takes off inland, thus avoiding the Ord of Caithness and

4025.

The station at Kyle of Lochalsh must surely be the most familiar image of all Highland Railway locations. It took the form of a central island passenger platform in the middle of a dedicated railway jetty. A ramp from the road gave access to the passenger station and freight traffic was handled outboard of the passenger platforms on both sides of the jetty, much of it being transhipment traffic to coastal steamers and the like, for which many quays were provided. It is hard to find just one view which sums it all up, but this official view is especially appealing, if only because it shows something of the environment, not least the Isle of Skye background. It is certainly pre-LMS, but given that the whole place was not created until 1897-8, the scene itself is very much that which would have been present at the time of the grouping. If truth be told (rail vehicle and ship cosmetics apart) it remained thus for the whole of the LMS period and is still recognisable in our present day and age. (LMS Official)

---

thence via the remote fastnesses of Sutherland and Caithness until it reaches the lower lying land of NE Caithness between Altnabreac and Georgemas Junction, at which latter point the Thurso branch connects with the line. As with the previous inland diversion, this line too, although following the easy Strath of Kildonan as far as Kinbrace and just beyond, still has to climb to make progress to the summit at the Sutherland and Caithness county boundary between Forsinard and Altnabreac.

It is all too easy to speculate why the Far North line made such dramatic inland deviations from what could have been the shorter alternatives. To have kept to the coast in either or both cases would undoubtedly have been more expensive 'mile for mile' in terms of construction costs, albeit technically quite feasible; and it is also arguable that fewer miles at a higher cost per mile would have been little if any more expensive in the long run. But this solution would also have deprived many remote places from rail facilities they have enjoyed for well over a century - and maybe that was the prime consideration. As it was, some modest degree of recompense for adopting the circuitous approach, whether it be on the Far North line itself, or closer to Inverness both south and west of Dingwall, was to lead to a number of branch lines being built in support of both of them - see Chapter 4.

Whatever the precise reasons for the system developing as it did, that is what the Highland bequeathed to the LMS in 1923 and it is hoped that this analysis of some of the factors, be they geographical or economic, which first determined their presence and actual location on the ground, will help readers understand the nature of the task which faced the LMS in 1923 - maybe even serving to explain some of the many solutions which the larger company offered.

The Highland Railway Infrastructure

Like most railways of the pre-1923 era, the Highland had its own way of doing things and some of these tended to be rather permanent in nature. Locomotives, carriages and wagons may well have changed over the years (see Chapter 5) but the basic ambience of the system was slower to adjust. Much of this was a reflection of the nature of the line itself as it developed and already covered above, from which it may well be deduced

Lairg was one of many modest settlements which may well never have had rail facilities at all but for the perambulations of the Far North line - see text. It was given restrained but adequate facilities - solid masonry on the main platform and typical pre-fabrication for the rest. But what is interesting in this case is that the single-storey stone buildings display a near-vernacular form which hints at the familiar 'Butt and Ben' style of many Scottish crofts. Whether or not this was deliberate will never be known, but it seemed to display that 'sense of place' which was typical of so many Highland stations.

(Peter Tatlow Collection)

Right: The Mound Junction in late LMS or, conceivably, early BR times when LMS upper quadrant signal arms had replaced the earlier Highland sentinels - main line to the left, Dornoch branch bay on the right. Compared with earlier days, the branch run-round had been shortened (the right foreground turnout was not there in pre-group days) but the facilities are still more than adequate and convey a clear impression of both care and activity.

(The late Gavin Wilson Collection)

(correctly) that because of the relative lack of too many imposing engineering features, the Highland never displayed the kind of distinctive house style in this field which other companies often adopted. It tended, to use a modern phrase, to 'go with the flow' of contemporary thinking and although there were many structures of a build quality which have survived until our present day, it is hard to find one which shouts 'Highland' above all else.

But other things were different. Perhaps the most obvious during LMS days, and an aspect which truly defined the origin of many of our pre-1923 lines for many a long year after the grouping, was the long survival of its highly distinctive signals and their associated signal cabins - note, by the way, that the HR preferred the word 'cabin' to the more ubiquitous 'box' used by most others....... From 1928 or thereabouts, the LMS began to institute standard signalling practices throughout its system, mostly by way of adopting upper quadrant semaphore arms in place of the previously universal lower quadrant types. This went hand-in-hand with a sort of semi-standardised location for the positioning of the signals themselves - dominantly to

The private station at Dunrobin Castle symbolised the direct participation and financial support of the Dukes of Sutherland in the promotion of railways in the far north. In the far distance can be seen the shed in which resided the Duke's private saloons and locomotive, a privilege enjoyed by him until the nationalisation of Britain's railways in 1948. The station still remains 'in situ', now devoid of all its sidings, but the Duke's own locomotive, the diminutive 0-4-4T Dunrobin, along with his small saloon, went to Canada many years ago. By great good fortune, his main saloon, the working prototype for HM King Edward VII's Royal Saloons of 1902, is preserved and on show at the National Railway Museum.

(The late Gavin Wilson Collection)

This panoramic view of Helmsdale, taken from the south in late LMS days, gives a very clear impression of how the main line, running right to left across the foreground, turns sharply inland again - see text. The coastal plain which the line could have followed, albeit rather narrow, is clearly apparent in the distance. This is the route followed by the A9 road alternative, just visible at the divide between the rising ground to the left of the picture and the coast plain itself.

(Author's collection)

the left of the running line on double track sections. Amongst other things, this was one reason for the LMS adopting left hand drive for all its standard locomotives during the 1920s, though for the Highland Section (almost wholly single track) this subtle refinement was an almost total irrelevance......

These changes took time to apply across the company as a whole and it is a matter of fact that it was never completed during LMS days. Naturally enough, the principal main lines (both in Scotland and England) took precedence and against this scenario it was not to be expected that the Highland lines

Characteristic features of the remote nature of the Far North line as it traverses the wilderness between Helmsdale and Georgemas. The first view shows the typical rudimentary shelter at Borrobol platform, similar examples being found at many such isolated places - but note the replacement upper quadrant LMS signals, rare enough anywhere at the time much less at such a remote location. The picture below shows one of the so-called 'snow blowers', near Forsinard as the line approaches the Sutherland and Caithness border. These features, intended to deflect the wind and keep the line clear of snow in winter, were a familiar feature of the line in many places: whether or not they always worked properly is another matter.

(M.Blakemore Collection, the late H.C.Casserley)

would merit high priority given their single track nature. *En passant*, it may be relevant to mention in context that even the famous ex-Midland Railway Settle and Carlisle double track main line retained almost a full complement of MR signals until 1947, many of them on the 'wrong side' of the line - sic! Thus it was that throughout the LMS period, the distinctive Highland signal posts with their tall finials were largely unaltered. There were several places where upper quadrant arms replaced the older type (standard LMS practice where total signal replacement was not called for) but for the most part, things changed but little.

A similar situation existed with stations. In due course, the LMS did come up with a few standard ideas which it adopted from time to time, perhaps the most notable being its new style of station nameboard c.1937 (the so-called 'Hawkseye' style, usually set at an angle to an approaching train). This went with a fairly common 'black letters on yellow background' paint treatment, even if the pre-group signs themselves were not replaced. But most Highland stations retained their original signs and the writer has been unable to find photographic confirmation of either of these ideas being widely adopted. The LMS also adopted standard colour schemes for station painting, mainly a dark brown and cream combination but occasionally using green and cream in country areas. This 'livery' was also used for many signal boxes if repainted at all and some Highland structures would certainly have been thus adorned - details unavailable.

But the essential durability of the inherited infrastructure was to ensure that little of significance really changed during LMS days on the Highland and this applied to architecture and also to basic track layouts for that matter. In neither of these cases, unlike many British companies (CR, GWR, LNWR, MR &c.), did the Highland show any real preferences for any one solution, preferring to adopt a largely conventional and essentially pragmatic approach in most situations, whether it be platform canopies, footbridges or whatever else may have been relevant. Thus, when it built an imposing station (of which it had more than a few) it tended to adopt a style in harmony with the locality rather than impose an alien form (eg Derby 'Gothick' in the high Pennines to quote but one!)

There was, of course, some degree of consistency between the appearance of stations where a particular stretch of line had been opened in one fell swoop, so to speak, but for the most part it was mostly done in a restrained and economic way. And in one particular respect, the Highland did stamp its presence more widely when it came to the smaller stations on the line. Here, purely for economic reasons, it regularly adopted pre-

Georgemas Junction in 1935, looking south on a wet day, Thurso branch to the right. Despite the dull weather, the flat and featureless terrain of this part of Caithness (see text) is more than apparent.

(Gavin Wilson Collection)

Evidence that LMS standard practices did permeate north to some extent is offered in this general view of Dingwall, taken from the south in the late 1930s and scarcely different from HR days. But lurking just to the right of the left hand steps of the footbridge can just be seen a new LMS 'Hawkseye' station sign in corporate black and yellow LMS colours. It is not known how widespread such new LMS practices were on the Highland, but the likelihood is that such as were to be seen were probably confined to full station repaints and/or major refurbishment of the total facilities.

(Author's collection)

Blair Atholl station (exact date unknown but certainly in LMS days) typified the restrained and dignified architectural style adopted by the Highland at many of its more important places. It was rare to find two alike, though from time to time there were some similarities - eg twin 'pavilions' flanking a central open-fronted colonnade with multiple pillars (as seen here) were a regular occurrence and will be seen in many other pictures elsewhere in this book. As far as is known, however, the rather impressive two-storey centre block at Blair Atholl behind the colonnade and between these pavilions was unique to this station and it was not at all uncommon to find other examples where the central treatment of an essentially similar concept tended to be unique to any one place.

The lattice footbridge and supporting buildings - eg the goods shed in the distance - were more standardised, the HR usually relying on outside contractors for its footbridges and using pre-fabricated techniques for much of the rest. But the effect was rarely less than harmonious and even in 2003, much of the basic Highland character remains intact wherever such structures have survived.

(The late Gavin Wilson)

fabricated structures of a highly standardised nature - usually vertical timber planks (joints covered with half round strips) and corrugated iron roofs - the so-called 'tin tabernacles' referred to earlier in this book. These mostly took the form of simple platform shelters at the more important double track passing places where something a bit better was offered on the other platform, but in some cases they formed the only covered facilities at remote locations. Other than signal cabins, these were probably the most typical of all Highland structures.

Even so, it is hard to make too many valid generalisations in either Highland or LMS days and the best I can therefore do is to use some of the space available to me in order to illustrate some of the great variety which could be seen.

LMS

3

Main Line Train Working

IT IS A MOOT POINT whether or not to start this rather more detailed review of the facilities offered by the LMS with the services for which engines and rolling stock were provided, or the actual running hardware itself. But since the former usually determined the nature of the latter, there is some logic in considering the services first. Since these can also reveal much of the nature of the railway itself, I make no apology for treating matters in this order.

The fundamental pattern of main line services in LMS days was very much a continued but ever-improving version of the three main areas of activity which appertained prior to the grouping. In prime position was the main line from Perth to Inverness (via both routes north of Aviemore), followed by the services north of Inverness - most of them for the Far North but not forgetting the Kyle route. All of these were now purely LMS in direct succession to the pre-group position, of course, but in addition to them was a rather important third element of quasi-main line activity - that to Keith along the south shores of the Moray Firth, which made connections at both this point and at Elgin with the GNSR (now LNER) sphere of influence.

These three routes will be considered separately for the most part, leaving the treatment of the various branches to a later chapter, using sub-headings for additional clarity and starting with passenger services along the Perth-Inverness spine. However, in all cases it is well to remember that the Highland was basically a single track system along most of its routes, save for a few exceptions - eg, but not exclusively, double track from Blair Atholl to Druimuachdar - and that 'main line' had a different connotation in these northern fastnesses to that which pertained to most parts of the LMS where double track was the 'norm', quadruple track was very common and duplicated routes were often available.

The following analyses are based on two different sample years, starting with the Public 1936 LMS summer timetable in the case of passenger services, chosen mainly because this was a time when the LMS had settled down and when changes, of which many had started soon after 1922, began to permeate more widely, not least in Scotland. But in the Highlands, this was mostly a matter of (some) new hardware rather than basic operating principle, the 1936 timetable being therefore quite typical of the general LMS approach on the Highland Section for quite some time both before and after that date.

Unfortunately, contemporary working timetables for freight trains are far more difficult to track down, never having been widely seen other than by those members of the railway staff who needed to know these things: "This timetable must be kept strictly private and must not be given to the public" was the printed warning on the title page - sic!. The vast majority of such documents have long been consigned to limbo but thanks to a very good friend of mine who lent me a copy of one of the rare survivors, I have been able to study the 1929 freight timetables for the whole of the ex-HR lines, from which, as far can be judged, they too seem to be reasonably typical of a longer period.

At the same time, although these specific sources form the basis of my analysis, it is important to enter the vital caveat that they can only reveal exact patterns for the years they represent. I have therefore used them mainly to establish the sort of principles which seem to have held good for a number of years. That changes took place over time is beyond doubt, but as far as I can determine, those on the ex-HR lines were more in the nature of 'fine-tuning' a long-established and proven way of doing things - largely on the "If it is not broken, don't mend it" principle - rather than anything more radical. In consequence, readers with access to similar documents from different years may well spot some of the more subtle changes which I do not have the space to cover in detail.

Passenger Services: Perth and Inverness

The main line north from Perth was, as already stated, the main trunk of the Highland system and its services reflected this fact. They can conveniently be divided into two main categories, namely through services along the whole distance (via either alternative north of Aviemore) and those shorter, all stations operations which covered but part of the route. If truth be told, the nature of the line north of Perth was such that the conventional image of the long-distance express (ie very few intermediate stops) was a rather rare creature north of Perth and it it was far more usual to encounter through services which served quite a few intermediate locations along the way. Nevertheless, they usually ran under 'express' headcodes and did not stop everywhere.

At Table I are listed the through services between Perth and Inverness during the summer of 1936, mostly in order of their departure time from Perth (northbound) or their time of arrival at Perth (southbound). The published timetable itself was very complex, being fully annotated with details of all through carriages both on the Highland network itself and to and from

These two evocative views, taken at the same location leaving Perth in the mid-1920s, fully encapsulate the nature of passenger trains on the Highland during the first few years after the grouping, illustrating as they do how quickly non-Highland carriages began to appear on the scene. In the first picture, Jones 4-4-0 No.14382, Loch Moy, is in charge of a five coach local to Blair Atholl. A late period Midland non-corridor third is at the front, followed by a Highland carriage. The third vehicle is possibly ex-Caledonian and the fourth ex-HR; but the only vehicle with guard's accommodation is an ex-LNWR bogie full brake at the rear, still in LNWR livery.

The second train of mostly gangwayed stock - service not specified but probably for Inverness - displays even more carriage variety. Headed by Drummond 'Castle' Class 4-6-0 No.14691 Brodie Castle (one of the three final examples built in 1917 with 6ft driving wheels and six-wheel tenders rather than the 5ft 9in wheels and eight-wheel tenders of the original sixteen examples), the carriages, from the front, are: Midland; Caledonian; LNWR; LMS standard; two LNWR; LMS standard; LNWR and LMS standard. Note that there are two LNWR full brakes in addition to the guard's van space in the first and third carriages in the train. However, there is no dining car and the locomotive carries the conventional local passenger headlamp code.

(M.Blakemore Collection; the late Gavin Wilson Collection)

This typically vast double-headed northbound cavalcade photographed in the mid-1920s near Luncarty (on the ex-Caledonian main line between Perth and Stanley Junction) is at least twelve carriages long and stated to be the 3.40pm down train from Perth, which had become the 3.55pm by 1936 (for details see Table I). The locomotives are Drummond 4-6-0 No.14682 Beaufort Castle (from the original series with 5ft 9in driving wheels) and Cumming 'Clan' Class 4-6-0 No.14764 Clan Munro. Apart from the leading LNWR corridor brake third, the carriage origins are hard to discern, but the usual variety is clearly present.

(The late Gavin Wilson Collection)

locations south of Perth. This was very much a feature of the way of doing things in those days and modern travellers would often be astonished to discover how many complex journeys could be made, either without change of carriage or by timed connections at many locations - would that we had similar facilities in our more modern era! I have done my best to include as many of these as possible, but would crave readers' indulgence should they know of any I have omitted.

Additionally, by way of preliminaries, it should perhaps be mentioned that outside the summer period, several of the trains

listed in Table I were combined, whereas in summer it was not at all unusual to run some trains in several parts, especially after the start of the grouse-shooting season. Finally, trains were regularly re-assembled at places like Aviemore and Perth before proceeding further. For simplicity's sake, these latter complications have mostly been omitted, but readers should be aware that this was a common way of doing things.

continued on page 38

TABLE I: THROUGH PASSENGER SERVICES PERTH-INVERNESS - SUMMER 1936

Monday-Saturday, save where noted. Sunday services were very few and are all given after the Southbound times. Arrival times in the 'Details' column are those at the final destination as given in the LMS timetable. This summary uses the 24 hour clock in line with modern custom

NORTHBOUND

Time	Details
00.55(MO)	**Perth-Inverness via Forres.** Arrived 05.12. Sleeping cars Glasgow to Inverness with some intermediate stops north of Aviemore. Through carriages Glasgow to Kyle and Wick
01.00(MX)	**Perth-Inverness via Carr Bridge.** Arrived 05.25. Train details as MO but non-stop Aviemore-Inverness
01.20(MX)	**Perth-Inverness via Carr Bridge.** Arrived 05.45. Divided at Aviemore: through coaches for Keith (arrived 07.15)
05.05	**Perth-Inverness via Carr Bridge.** Ran from 7th July, arrived 08.45. **'THE ROYAL HIGHLANDER'**, through carriages and sleeping cars from Euston (Dep 19.20). Dining car from Perth to Inverness. Scheduled to stop only at Aviemore, but by prior notification thereafter
05.30	**Perth-Inverness via Forres.** Arrived 10.52. Through carriages and sleeping cars London-Inverness. Stopped at virtually all stations north of Pitlochry, some by prior notification
06.25	**Perth-Inverness via Carr Bridge.** Arrived 09.50. Dining car Perth-Inverness. Divided at Aviemore: sections for Inverness via Carr Bridge (non-stop including dining car and TPO) and Inverness via Forres (all stations). Connected at Aviemore with all stations from Newtonmore to Inverness via Carr Bridge - see Table II
09.30	**Perth-Inverness via Carr Bridge.** Arrived 13.47. Stopped almost all stations, some conditional. Detached carriages at Ballinluig for Aberfeldy and Aviemore for all stations via Forres (arrived Inverness 14.45). Dining car Perth-Inverness via Carr Bridge
11.55	**Perth-Inverness via Carr Bridge.** Arrived 15.38. Through carriages Glasgow-Inverness via both Carr Bridge and Forres, also from Glasgow to Keith. Through carriages Edinburgh to Inverness via Carr Bridge; dining car Glasgow-Aviemore. Ran FSX until 29th August, thereafter daily. Stopped at Pitlochry and Kingussie only south of Aviemore, thereafter almost all stations on both routes - see also Table II
12.05(FSO)	**Perth-Inverness via Forres.** Arrived 16.45; ran until 29th August. Through carriages Glasgow to Inverness and Keith, also Edinburgh to Inverness. Dining car to Aviemore. Non-stop to Kingussie then most stations from there onwards.
12.10	**Perth-Inverness via Forres.** Arrived 17.57. All stations. Through carriages Glasgow and Edinburgh to Inverness
15.55	**Perth-Inverness via Carr Bridge.** Arrived 19.55. Through Carriages Glasgow-Inverness and Edinburgh-Inverness via both Carr Bridge and Forres; through carriage Perth-Aberfeldy (SX); dining car Perth-Inverness. Stopped at most stations south of Aviemore and all stations thereafter (some conditional) - see also Table II
16.05(SO)	**Perth-Inverness via Forres.** Arrived 21.22. Through carriages Glasgow-Inverness; Edinburgh-Inverness and Perth-Inverness, all via Forres, were taken off the 15.55 (above) to form this SO train; dining car throughout. All stations from Ballinluig onwards except Killiecrankie and Auldearn
18.05	**Perth-Inverness via Carr Bridge.** Arrived 21.40. Through train and dining car Glasgow-Inverness - non-stop from Aviemore. Connection at Aviemore for Boat of Garten and Grantown-on-Spey only - Forres and Nairn via Inverness

A fascinating combination of ex-MR arc-roof six-wheel lavatory third plus an almost brand new LMS standard brake third formed what is stated on the original print to be the 'down breakfast' at Luncarty in the 1920s. Precisely what was meant is not known but it could be the very early morning train to Struan (Table II), which may explain the unusual absence of first class accommodation. The featured locomotive is 4-4-0 No.14384 Loch Laggan.   (Author's collection)

SOUTHBOUND

08.30   **Inverness-Perth via Carr Bridge.** Arrived 11.51. Through train and dining car Inverness-Glasgow plus through carriages from Kyle of Lochalsh. Through carriages from Keith and Nairn attached at Aviemore

09.55 **   **Inverness-Perth via Forres.** Arrived 15.15. Through carriages Inverness-Glasgow, Inverness-Edinburgh and Keith-Glasgow. Dining car Aviemore-Perth. Stopped at most stations both north and south of Aviemore

11.05 **   **Inverness-Perth via Carr Bridge.** Arrived 14.56. Through carriages and dining car Inverness-Glasgow; through carriages Inverness-Edinburgh. Stopped all stations to Aviemore, then Kingussie, Blair Atholl and Pitlochry only

15.20   **Inverness-Perth via Carr Bridge.** Arrived 19.00.. Ran until 15th August only. Stopped at Aviemore, Newtonmore, Blair Atholl only, dining car from Aviemore

14.10 ##   **Inverness-Perth via Forres.** Arrived 21.52. Through carriages to Glasgow and Edinburgh; dining car Inverness-Perth only.. Through carriages Keith-Perth attached at Aviemore

15.45 ##   **Inverness-Perth via Carr Bridge.** Arrived 21.20. Through carriages Wick and Inverness to Glasgow; TPO Helmsdale-Perth; dining car from Aviemore to Glasgow

16.15 @@   **Inverness-Perth via Carr Bridge.** Arrived 20.20 and ran from 17th August only. Through carriages and sleeping cars Inverness-Euston. Attached through carriages and sleeping cars for Euston (from Gollanfield Jct via Forres) at Aviemore - see Table IV. Dining car Aviemore-Carstairs only.

16.35 @@   **Inverness-Perth via Carr Bridge.** Arrived 20.46. Through carriages and sleeping cars Inverness-Euston and Inverness-King's Cross; dining car Inverness-Perth. Many conditional stops.

j20.10(SO)   **Inverness-Perth via Carr Bridge.** Arrived 00.13. Stopped at all stations to Ballinluig except Killiecrankie

23.20(SX)   **Inverness-Perth via Carr Bridge.** Arrived 04.20. Through carriages and sleeping cars Inverness-Glasgow. Forres and Nairn served via Inverness

** These trains were remarshalled and made cross-connections at Aviemore between 12.11 and 12.38, whence the 11.05 ex-Inverness proceeded ahead of the 09.55

These trains were remarshalled and made cross-connections at Aviemore between 16.48 and 16.58, whence the 15.45 ex-Inverness proceeded ahead of the 14.10

@@ One or other of these trains would have included the return working of 'THE ROYAL HIGHLANDER' stock, though neither was named as such

SUNDAYS

09.40   **Perth-Inverness via Forres.** Arrived 13.57. Through carriages Glasgow-Inverness. Dining car throughout - ran mainly to connect with overnight trains from the south.

16.10   **Inverness-Perth via Carr Bridge.** Arrived 19.45. Through carriages Inverness-Glasgow, dining car to Perth. Called at Tomatin on request - sic!

16.05   **Inverness-Perth via Forres.** Arrived 20.20. Through carriages Inverness-Glasgow, dining car to Perth

Southbound at Luncarty in the 1920s, probably mid-to-late afternoon, with Loch Laggan piloting an unidentified 'Castle' from the 6ft driving wheel series. The unidentified train is yet again a typically mixed formation and, speculating a little, could perhaps be the service which in 1936 left Inverness at 11.05am - Table I. The leading coach is ex-North British, certainly bound for Edinburgh. On the original print, a Pullman dining car can clearly be distinguished as the eighth vehicle in the train. (Author's collection)

From these services, a few basic facts can be noted. Firstly, it is abundantly clear that both lines north of Aviemore were very adequately served. Those trains which were routed via Dava and Forres (in either direction) naturally took longer in transit than those via the shorter Carr Bridge route, which was the main choice for most of the through trains. But a very determined effort was always made to ensure that integration of the two routes was fully achieved at Aviemore, be it north or southbound. This sort of approach undoubtedly added to the overall cost of operation, not least in the provision of extra locomotive power and carriages to serve both routes, but it is a real measure of the generally enlightened LMS attitude to such things that there was never any hint that the longer route (along with its many intermediate stations) should be 'short-changed'.

Traditional through carriages and sleeping cars to and from England continued much as in the pre-group days. After 1922, the LMS indulged in a bit of rationalisation between its own two competing routes (West Coast and Midland) by cutting out the Midland option and it would not have been surprising had it tried to discourage East Coast traffic altogether! But this did not happen and it is clear from a detailed study of the timetable itself (and its many 'small print' annotations) that connecting services and through carriages were provided to serve many routes beyond Perth. It is thought, for example, that the bulk of through services to Edinburgh used LNER stock, a fact which is confirmed photographically in some cases. It should also be mentioned that the Edinburgh through services used the LNER Waverley station not the LMS equivalent at Princes Street.

What is also worth noting is that by the mid-1930s, the LMS had not only added catering provision to its overnight trains north of Perth wherever the timings were appropriate - ie late afternoon/early evening southbound departures or early morning in the opposite direction - but had also introduced dining cars on almost all the daytime through trains between Perth and Inverness. This improvement actually commenced in the 1920s, prior to which the Highland main line had not seen too much of this sort of thing. It never had its own dining cars, for example, such catering vehicles as ventured north of Perth (very few) being the property of those companies with which it connected, including Pullman which had ten years of a residual contract with the Caledonian Railway left to run when the LMS was formed and actually began to send cars to Aviemore from Glasgow in 1922.

When taken with the additional provision of corridor stock for longer distance use after 1922, it can be seen that the LMS made significant improvements to the passenger environment - and this enhancement was also to be extended elsewhere on the former Highland system as we shall soon see.

Meantime, the more purely local 'all stations' services between Perth and Inverness remained more than adequate as Table II reveals. These trains, operating over only part of the route, were additional to the through services. Transit times were not exactly rapid for there were very many stops, not to mention numerous steep gradients and the need for trains to be held at passing stations to enable through trains to pass. Four hours or slightly more was the norm for even the fastest trains on the shorter 118 mile route between Perth and Inverness via Carr Bridge and at least an hour more via Forres. But given that many of the through trains also stoppped at a fair number of small intermediate stations, often by prior request, it can be seen that at a time when personal mobility was by no means as common as in our own time, the main spine of the Highland main line was by no means ill served as far as the local needs of the resident population were concerned.

TABLE II: INTERMEDIATE PASSENGER SERVICES PERTH-INVERNESS - SUMMER 1936

Monday-Saturday, save where noted - no Sunday services. Arrival times in the 'Details' column are those at the final destination as given in the LMS public timetable. This summary uses the 24 hour clock in line with modern custom

NORTHBOUND

Time	Details
05.45	**Perth-Struan.** Arrived 07.55. All stations except Luncarty and Guay. Called on request at Guay to set down
07.45	**Aviemore - Grantown-on-Spey.** Arrived 08.10. All stations
08.00	**Newtonmore-Aviemore.** Arrived 08.30. All stations
09.00	**Aviemore-Inverness via Forres.** Arrived 11.15. All stations. Combines at Forres with train from Keith (Table IV)
09.05	**Aviemore-Inverness via Carr Br.** Arrived 10.28. All stations
09.40	**Perth-Blair Atholl.** Arrived 10.54. All stations save Luncarty
14.33	**Aviemore-Inverness via Forres.** Arrived 16.40. FSX until 29th August, daily from 31st August. All stations except Dava and Allanfearn
13.48(SO)	**Perth-Blair Atholl.** Arrived 15.13. All stations save Luncarty
16.25	**Blair Atholl-Struan.** Arrived 16.35
16.00(SX)	**Perth-Blair Atholl.** Arrived 17.23. All stations
16.20(SO)	**Perth-Blair Atholl.** Arrived 17.41. All stations
18.55(SX)	**Aviemore-Inverness via Forres.** Arrived 21.05. All stations. Received through carriages from Glasgow and Edinburgh off the 15.55 ex-Perth - see Table I.
20.05	**Perth-Blair Atholl.** Arrived 21.23. To Struan(SO), arrived 21.34. All stations except Luncarty and Guay but called on request at both to set down
20.52	**Aviemore - Grantown-on-Spey.** Arrived 21.14. Stopped at Boat of Garten only
22.40(SO)	**Perth-Blair Atholl.** Arrived 23.54. All stations save Guay, Killiecrankie. Called on request at Guay to set down

SOUTHBOUND

Time	Details
06.50	**Blair Atholl-Perth.** Arrived 08.19. All stations save Luncarty
08.24	**Grantown-on-Spey - Aviemore.** Arrived 08.44. Stopped at Boat of Garten only
08.40	**Struan-Perth.** Arrived 10.12. All stations except Luncarty
07.45	**Nairn-Aviemore.** Arrived 09.26. Through carriages from Keith. All stations except Auldearn. Through carriages attached at Aviemore to the 08.30 ex-Inverness - see Table I
09.05	**Inverness-Forres.** Arrived 09.56. All stations, thence to Keith (see Table IV)
13.28	**Blair Atholl-Perth.** Arrived 14.45. All stations save Luncarty
15.25	**Gollanfield Jct-Aviemore via Forres.** Arrived 17.17. Ran from 17th August only (using empty carriage stock sent from Inverness). All stations excepty Auldearn and Brodie. Through carriages and sleeping cars to Euston, attached to 16.15 ex-Inverness at Aviemore - see Table I
17.00	**Struan-Perth.** Arrived 18.34. All stations
15.30	**Inverness-Aviemore via Forres.** Arrived 18.24. All stations
17.20	**Inverness-Aviemore via Carr Br.** Arrived 18.37. All stations
18.40	**Aviemore-Newtonmore.** Arrived 19.14. All stations, formed by combining the 15.30 and 17.20 from Inverness at Aviemore
20.15(SO)	**Blair Atholl-Perth.** Arrived 21.39. All stations save Luncarty; through carriages to Dundee
21.25(SO)	**Grantown-on-Spey - Aviemore.** Arrived 21.47. Non stop

However, one thing remained totally consistent after 1922 and applied to all routes, not just the Perth-Inverness main line. Sunday was a genuine 'day of rest' in those times and was probably observed rather more strictly north of the border than elsewhere in Britain. Accordingly, although special excursions were not precluded, no timetabled trains ran at all on that day, save for a handful, operated solely to make connections with longer distance through services to or from locations outwith the Highland sphere of influence. One senses that even these were operated rather grudgingly and such alternatives as were available on Sundays by road (or sea in some cases) were not exactly encouraged if the following verbatim extract from the LMS timetable is any guide:

"The following information is inserted for the benefit of the Public and the Company are not in any way responsible for the accuracy of said information, nor do they guarantee the running of Coaches, Motors or Steamers, nor do they accept liability for any loss or injury arising to Passengers by said Coaches, Motors and Steamers............"

This exhortation applied across the board, no matter the day of the week, but a further annotation is even more revealing:

"For Highland Transport Company's Sunday Bus Service North of Inverness, see page 590. Railway Tickets are not available by these Buses."

This note appears on the timetable page for the Far North and Kyle lines where, with one sole exception, the railway closed down completely on Sunday; and it is these fascinating routes which will next be considered.

Passenger Services: North of Inverness

The celebrated routes north of Inverness were, by quite some margin, far longer than the Perth-Inverness line, for if one adds the Far North route (just over 161 miles) to the more than 63 miles between Dingwall and Kyle of Lochalsh, the resultant mileage (c.225) well exceeded that of either of the main routes south of Inverness. Collectively, they also represented what was probably the longest wholly single track operation under sole ownership to be seen anywhere in Britain.

The routes diverged some 18-19 miles north of Inverness at Dingwall which, in relation to this part of the system, played much the same sort of pivotal role as did Aviemore further south. The passenger services are summarised at Table III from which it can readily be seen that by far the bulk of the traffic was to or from the Far North line. But the Kyle line was not ignored; in fact, it enjoyed one more through service along its whole length to and from Dingwall (seven per day) than the six trains only which served the full Inverness-Wick route.

As with services south of Inverness, there were numerous detailed annotations to the timetables and I have included as many of these as possible consistent with keeping the summary reasonably straightforward. But, as previously mentioned, it is not possible to guarantee that all variations have been included and apologies are offered for any significant omissions.

LMS Standard Class 4F 0-6-0 No.4317 is seen here with an up local at Pitlochry c.1938. After the arrival of Class 5 4-6-0s (see Chapter 5), the 4Fs, which were never too popular anyway, were not especially widespread on the Highland main line and more often seen on goods trains. The carriages are a somewhat tidy set by contemporary LMS standards: the first two are of Caledonian origin, the third is LMS standard, but the coach at the rear is not positively identified.

(Peter Tatlow Collection)

TABLE III: INVERNESS-KYLE OF LOCHALSH & FAR NORTH - SUMMER 1936

Monday-Saturday, save where noted. No Sunday services except southbound at 13.00 Lairg-Inverness, arriving 15.41 and stopping at most stations. Arrival times in the 'Details' column are those at the final destination as given in the LMS public timetable. This summary uses the 24 hour clock in line with modern custom

NORTHBOUND

Time	Details
06.05	**Inverness-Tain.** Arrived 07.56. Stopped all stations except Bunchrew and Lentran
06.45	**Inverness-Wick. 'THE ORCADIAN'.** Arrived 12.54. Limited stops to Tain, then all stations. Dining car Inverness-The Mound; through carriages to Thurso, Glasgow-Wick
07.25	**Inverness-Kyle of Lochalsh. 'THE HEBRIDEAN'.** Arrived 10.33. Beauly and all stations except save Conon, Glencarron, Attadale and Duirinish. Dining car Inverness-Kyle of Lochalsh
09.20	**Inverness-Tain.** Arrived 11.15. All stations
09.48	**Inverness-Lairg.** Arrived 12.20. 24th July-11th August only. Beauly, Dingwall and all stations save Foulis, Delny and Nigg
10.15	**Inverness-Kyle of Lochalsh. 'THE LEWISMAN'.** Arrived 13.40. Clunes, Beauly, Conon then all stations (some conditional). Dining car Inverness-Kyle of Lochalsh. Steamer connections for Portree and Stornoway. This service is noted as not conveying motor cars, for which a separate train ran from Strathcarron to Kyle of Lochalsh at 11.55
10.25	**Inverness-Wick.** Arrived 16.29. Almost all stations (many of them conditional). Dining car Inverness-Helmsdale; through carriages Inverness-Thurso
14.40	**Inverness-Helmsdale.** Arrived 18.56. All stations
16.15	**Inverness-Wick. 'THE JOHN O' GROAT'.** Arrived 21.10. Stopped at Dingwall, Tain and Bonar Bridge only, thereafter limited stops. Dining car Inverness-Wick; through carriages Inverness-Thurso also Inverness-Strathpeffer and possibly Inverness-Dornoch (FSO) until late August
16.52	**Dingwall-Kyle of Lochalsh.** Arrived 19.20. All stations. Stock received off 16.15 ex-Inverness. *Ran as a mixed train - see text*
17.00	Inverness-Tain. Arrived 18.50. All stations
18.05	Inverness-Tain. Arrived 19.46. All stations
20.15	Inverness-Tain. Arrived 20.05. All stations
22.40(SO)	Inverness-Dingwall. Arrived 23.25. All stations

SOUTHBOUND

Time	Details
05.00	**Kyle of Lochalsh-Inverness. 'THE LEWISMAN'.** Arrived 08.10. Limited stops; through carriages Kyle of Lochalsh-Glasgow. Connected with overnight steamer from Stornoway but had no dining car facilities
08.05	**Dingwall-Inverness.** Arrived 08.53. All stations
06.10	**Kyle of Lochalsh-Dingwall.** Arrived 09.23. All stations save Duirinish and Attadale. Connected at Dingwall with 06.10 Helmsdale-Inverness. *Ran as a mixed train - see text*
06.10	**Helmsdale-Inverness.** Arrived 10.42. All stations except Loth
10.45	**Kyle of Lochalsh-Inverness. 'THE HEBRIDEAN'.** Arrived 14.20. All stations to Dingwall, thence at Muir of Ord only. Connected with steamer from Portree; dining car Kyle of Lochalsh-Inverness
12.40	**Tain-Inverness.** Arrived 14.38. All stations
08.45	**Wick-Inverness.** Arrived 15.00. All stations to Tain, thence Invergordon and Dingwall only. Dining car The Mound-Inverness (received off the down 'ORCADIAN'); through carriages Thurso-Inverness, Wick-Glasgow and from Dornoch to Inverness (MSO until late August)
13.30	**Tain-Invergordon.** Arrived 13.58. All stations; forward at 14.30 from Invergordon - below
10.10	**Wick-Inverness. 'THE JOHN O' GROAT'.** Arrived 15.20. Limited stops to Invergordon, then Dingwall only; dining car Wick-Inverness; through carriages Thurso-Inverness
14.30	**Invergordon-Inverness.** Arrived 15.54. All stations
16.00	**Tain-Inverness.** Arrived 17.54. All stations
17.40	**Kyle of Lochalsh-Inverness.** Arrived 21.06. All stations to Beauly, then non stop. Dining car Kyle of Lochalsh-Inverness
15.40	**Wick-Inverness. 'THE ORCADIAN'.** Arrived 21.17. Called all stations to Tain, then Dingwall only. Dining car Helmsdale-Inverness (received off 10.25 down train); through carriages Thurso-Inverness
20.05	**Tain-Inverness.** Arrived 21.50. All stations

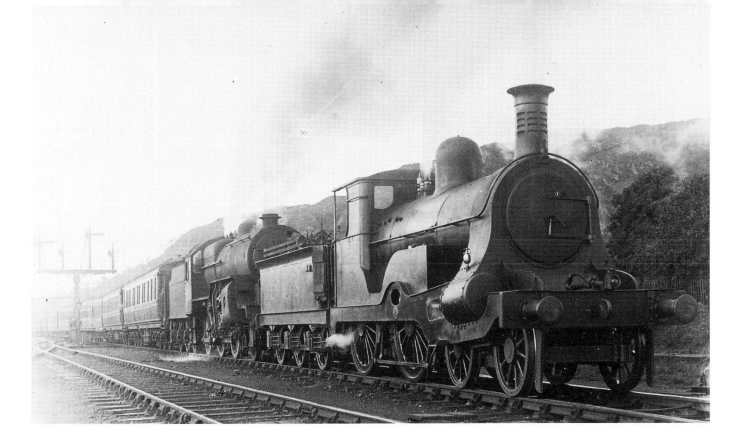

In effect, the greater use of the Far North line north of Dingwall arose mostly in consequence of additional services to and from locations between Tain and Helmsdale, the former being particularly well served, both on its own account and by virtue of all the through trains stopping there. Furthermore, Dingwall itself had at least a dozen services every day to and from Inverness - far better than many a location in our modern day come to think about it. Moreover, what is also worthy of comment is the extent to which the LMS, at a time when fiscal constraints were an ever-present consideration for the railways in general, managed to maintain such a comprehensive service in this remote and sparsely populated area.

One or two points may further serve to emphasise this fact, one of which is the rather clever way in which the use of dining cars was organised so as to provide refreshments on almost all through services to and from Inverness, the 05.00 from The Kyle being the principal exception. This was often achieved by detaching the dining car at intermediate locations so as to enable it to be attached to a service in the opposite direction. This was mostly on the Far North route as noted in Table III, but it is also worth noting that outside the summer period covered in the table, it was common for dining cars on the Kyle route to be transferred between down and up trains at Achnasheen. This practice, continuing well into BR days, also allowed a slight reduction of the number of dining cars during the less busy seasons, thus allowing essential maintenance of these more complex carriages to take place.

Additionally interesting is the introduction by the LMS of a series of fine and appropriate train names for its main services north of Inverness. Passengers always liked their trains to be thus distinguished in those days for it gave a 'sense of occasion'

This extraordinary combination of motive power (Jones 'Strath' Class 'Crewe-type' 4-4-0 plus LMS standard 2-6-0) was seen c.1930. Sadly, the location, date and locomotive details are not recorded, nor is the train specified; but the most unusual nature of the picture justifies its inclusion. The first two carriages are ex-WCJS twelve-wheel sleeping cars and a dining car is seen as the second vehicle to the left of the signal post. The central position of the lamp on the front of the 4-4-0 is not a recognised passenger head code and is likely to be a red tail lamp carried during a shunting manoevre. (Michael Blakemore Collection)

to their journey, not least by way of the distinctive headboards sometimes mounted on the carriages. The LMS did not always pay due attention to the latter point (sic!) but was not slow to react to the general idea, offering many named trains along its whole system from the late 1920s onwards.

Finally, mention should also be made at this stage of that distinctive survival from Highland days, the 'Mixed' train. These were very commonly seen during pre-grouping years, but slowly became confined to the branch lines after 1922: we shall meet them again in Chapter 4. However, the Kyle of Lochalsh saw an exception to this general trend, by virtue of the fact that the one daily return service between there and Dingwall which did not go through to Inverness traditionally ran as a mixed train during LMS times.

Although, as far as I can determine, this seems to have been the only official main line mixed train at the time, it was by no means uncommon for passenger trains to carry goods traffic in

TABLE IV: INVERNESS-KEITH - SUMMER 1936

NOTES: 1. Monday-Saturday, save where noted. The few Sunday trains are given after the Westbound times. Arrival times in the 'Details' column are those at the final destination as given in the LMS public timetable. This summary uses the 24 hour clock in line with modern custom

2. ** Trains to or from the main line south via Forres, or with portions for that line.

3. ## Services referred to as 'LNER Train' beyond Elgin and worked by LNER to and from there. Most (all?) are thought to have employed LNER stock - see text

EASTBOUND

Time	Details
06.00	**Forres-Keith.** Arrived 07.15. All stations except Kinloss and Mosstowie
07.45 **	**Nairn-Forres.** Arrived 08.00. All stations except Aldearn, thence to Aviemore - see Table II
07.55 ##	**Inverness-Keith.** Arrived 10.05; Elgin 09.19 (ten minutes later FO). All stations. LNER connection for Aberdeen at Elgin (departed 09.32). Other LNER connections at Elgin and Keith
09.05	**Inverness-Keith.** Arrived 11.38. All stations
09.55 **	**Inverness-Forres.** Arrived 10.40. All stations except Allanfearn, Dalcross and Auldearn, thence to Perth - Table I
11.15	**Inverness-Keith.** Arrived 12.55, thence to Aberdeen using LMS Dual-Braked stock. Stopped Gollanfield Jct, Nairn, Forres, Elgin and Orbliston Jct only
13.00 ##	**Inverness-Keith.** Arrived 15.00; Elgin 14.10. Stopped all stations except Allanfearn, Dalcross, Auldearn and Mosstowie. LNER through carriages and dining car Inverness-Aberdeen, detached Elgin and worked by LNER from there (dep. 14.25). Connections for other LNER services at both Elgin and Keith
14.10 **	**Inverness-Keith.** Arrived 17.08. All stations. Also conveyed through carriages for Perth via Dava - see Table I - and waited at Forres for connections from Perth via Dava
15.25 **	**Gollanfield Jct-Forres.** Arrived 15.50. Ran from 17th August using empty carriage stock from Inverness. Non-stop Nairn-Forres, then to Aviemore via Dava. Through carriages and sleeping cars to Euston, attached to 16.15 ex-Inverness at Aviemore - see Tables I and II
15.30	**Inverness-Keith.** Arrived 17.30. All stations, thence to Aberdeen - LMS stock. Connections at Elgin and Keith with LNER services
16.22(SX)	**Inverness-Fort George.** Arrived 16.53. Ran from 24th August
18.05 ##	**Inverness-Elgin.** Arrived 19.17. All stations except Mosstowie. To Aberdeen - LMS and LNER stock on alternate days and worked from Elgin by LNER (dep. 19.25) with connections there for other LNER locations
19.15(SX)	**Inverness-Keith.** Departed 19.30(SO). Arrived 21.40(SX); 21.46(SO). All stations except Mosstowie.
20.00(ThO)	**Inverness-Keith.** Arrived 21.31. Semi-fast until 3rd September. Stopped at Nairn, Forres and Elgin only. LNER connection at Keith for Aberdeen (arrived 22.52)
22.10(SX)	**Inverness-Forres.** Departed 22.30(SO). Arrived 22.58(SX); 23.23(SO). All stations

WESTBOUND

04.28(MO)	**Forres-Inverness.** Arrived 05.12. Stopped Nairn only (** ex-Perth at 00.55 - see Table I)
06.15(MX)	**Forres-Nairn.** Arrived 06.35. Non-stop (** ex-Perth at 01.20 - see Table I)
06.35	**Keith-Inverness.** Arrived 08.55. From Aberdeen (dep. 04.35) using LMS stock. All stations.
09.55	**Forres-Inverness.** Arrived 10.52. From 7th July, all stations
08.50	**Keith-Inverness.** Arrived 11.15. All stations, connections from LNER at Keith. ** Attached through carriages from Aviemore at Forres (see Table II). **Note:** In 1938, this train conveyed through carriage(s) Keith-Glasgow, detached Forres. It is not known if this was also the case in 1936
10.15 ##	**Elgin-Inverness.** Arrived 11.34. All stations except Kinloss, Dalcross and Allanfearn. LNER through carriages and dining car from Aberdeen (dep. 07.50), worked by LNER to Elgin.
12.10	**Keith-Inverness.** Arrived 14.24. From Aberdeen (dep. 09.45), using LMS stock. All stations. LNER connections at Keith
13.45	**Forres-Inverness.** Arrived 14.45. All stations and conveyed through carriages to Perth via Inverness (** This train was ex-Perth at 09.30 - see Table I)
13.21(ThO)	**Keith-Inverness.** Arrived 15.05. From Aberdeen (dep. 11.50); Semi-fast until 3rd September. Stopped at Elgin, Forres and Nairn only. Other LNER connections at Keith
15.17(SX)	**Fort George-Inverness.** Arrived 16.12. Ran from 24th August
13.45	**Keith-Inverness.** Arrived 16.40. All stations except Allanfearn, LNER connections at Keith. Waited Forres: 52 min
15.40	**Keith-Inverness.** Arrived 17.57. All stations. LNER connections at Keith
17.05 ##	**Elgin-Inverness.** Arrived 18.20. All stations except Mosstowie and Kinloss. Through carriages from Aberdeen (dep. 14.20). LMS/LNER stock on alternate days; worked by LNER to Elgin
18.45(SO)	**Keith-Inverness.** Arrived 20.59. All stations, LNER connections at Keith
18.45(SX)	**Keith-Inverness.** Arrived 21.05. All stations except Auldearn. LNER connections at Keith. ** Combined at Forres with train from south via Dava (ex-Aviemore at 18.55 - see Table II)
20.30(SO)	**Forres-Inverness.** Arrived 21.22. All stations (** ex-Perth at 16.05 - see Table I)
20.30	**Keith-Inverness.** Arrived 22.03. From Aberdeen (dep. 18.45), using LMS stock. Stopped Elgin, Forres and Nairn only

SUNDAYS

13.14	**Forres-Inverness.** Arrived 13.57. Stopped only at Nairn (** ex-Perth at 09.40 - see Table I)
13.21	**Keith-Inverness.** Arrived 14.54. From Aberdeen (dep. 11.50). Ran July/August only, stopping Elgin, Forres and Nairn only
16.05 **	**Inverness-Forres.** Arrived 16.44. Stopped only at Nairn. Through dining car train to Perth and Glasgow - see Table I
19.30	**Inverness-Keith.** Arrived 21.05. To Aberdeen (arr. 22.34). Ran July/August only, stopping Nairn, Forres and Elgin only.

---

vehicles whose automatic braking systems allowed them to be marshalled with passenger-carrying stock. These included mail coaches, milk vans and all manner of vehicles whose cargo merited the faster transit time which passenger trains could offer. These types were usually referred to as 'Non-Passenger Coaching Stock' and this aspect of operation will be considered further when freight services are analysed later in the chapter.

Passenger Services: Inverness and Keith

The main line east from Inverness along the south shore of the Moray Firth was an important early part of the Highland, some parts of it having been actively promoted to prevent the GNSR reaching Inverness on its own metals. As can be seen from the system map offered on the back cover of this book, the many

Drummond 'Castle' Class 4-6-0 No.14687 Brahan Castle is seen crossing the steel truss Calvine viaduct near Struan in 1929 - the bridge was built when the line was doubled between 1898 and 1900. The train is unidentified but the leading coach is of former North Eastern Railway origin, probably bound for Edinburgh, the next two being ex-LNWR. The locomotive is seen in rather scruffy 1928 livery which, given the date of the picture, may still be red: it is certainly lined out. Brahan Castle is one of a few ex-HR types known to have been given the red livery with new style handpainted insignia in 1928 before the later adoption of lined black.

(Peter Tatlow Collection)

ramifications of this policy resulted in a veritable cat's cradle of rival HR and GNSR lines in the region between Elgin and Keith, to which the LMS and LNER fell heirs in 1923. To be fair to both companies, by this time they seem mostly to have forgotten the intense and often bitter HR/GNSR rivalry of the 19th Century and collaborated in offering a reasonable service. Table IV offers the LMS part of this operation.

Along with its LNER continuation from Keith, the main spine of this route formed an essential link between Inverness and Aberdeen, and its role, albeit long reduced in importance after the direct route south was built, was to remain significant throughout LMS times. Naturally enough, the Aberdeen traffic dominated, though the LMS did not work it beyond Keith.. Most trains terminated there and although there were through carriages, none of them seem to have ventured south of Aberdeen. Much reliance was also placed in the many complicated connections available at Keith and Elgin.

The latter location served mainly to provide connections to the many minor lines and branches in what might be called the LMS/LNER 'buffer zone', functioning as a regular changeover point between LMS and LNER motive power, the latter having its own independent route between there and Keith. In general, the through carriages (or trains) between Inverness and Aberdeen alternated, more or less, between LMS and LNER stock, and although the LMS timetable does not distinguish between them too clearly, it is likely that trains which changed engines at Elgin rather than Keith (usually referred to in the LMS timetable as 'LNER train' beyond Elgin) included all of those which used LNER stock, albeit probably augmented by LMS vehicles from time to time on its own part of the route. These have been annotated in the accompanying table as far as

possible. By contrast, those trains which used LMS stock seem to have changed engines at Keith. But it was the LNER which provided stock for the one through dining car train which made a daily out and back trip from Aberdeen to Inverness.

Further complicating matters on this route was the need to provide services between Inverness and Forres in connection with the main route south via Dava. These were a mixture of through trains which did not venture onto the Forres-Keith section at all and through carriages attached or detached at Forres to or from routine Inverness-Keith trains. Details of these have been included in Table IV and in some cases should be read in conjunction with information at Tables I and II.

Although perhaps ranking third in importance in the overall scheme of things as far as the Highland network as a whole was concerned, it can be seen that the 55 miles of main line between Inverness and Keith (again mostly single track) was every bit as complex an operation as the longer routes already covered and, as Table IV reveals, was by no means ill-served in terms of services, save on Sundays, of course, where the usual almost total shut-down took place.......

Freight Services: A few preliminaries

Although freight services will be considered under the same three route categories already used for passenger workings, it is thought helpful to make a few preliminary comments about those aspects of freight working on the Highland lines in general which apply to them all, if only to avoid repetition.

In our present day and age (written in 2003) it is almost impossible to conceive that there was once a time when freight revenue represented some two thirds of total railway earnings; yet such it was on both the LMS and LNER systems. It should

Here, it is important to remember that the basic unit of operation was the individual (ie single) goods wagon, no matter how mechanically primitive it may have been. It was the means whereby any trader, no matter how small, who had reason to import or export commercial goods of any kind, could gain access to or from a broader market. In other words, almost any sort of trader could have need for the railway in one way or another. It thus follows that almost every station on the line would also need to have some sort of facility whereby goods could be loaded or unloaded, leaving local distribution by road (usually over relatively short distances) to the choice of the particular customer.

This basic *modus operandi* led to an almost nationwide tradition of different types of goods train according to function - and the Highland lines were no exception. At the bottom of the pecking order was the local goods train which would stop everywhere, collecting or delivering wagons of purely local concern as appropriate. Often called the 'pick-up' goods, it was almost always a daily event and referred to in LMS working rules as "Freight train stopping at intermediate stations." I have used the simpler phrase 'Ordinary Freight' to identify this sort of train in the accompanying tables.

This 1935 view shows the still fairly new Class 5 4-6-0 No.5013 at Druimuachdar with a northbound express. It is not the sharpest of pictures but is of considerable interest in that it can be related quite closely to the details given in Table I. By the mid-1930s, the principal express trains were getting a bit tidier in appearance (sic!) and apart from two ex-LNWR types (vehicles one and four), the rest of the carriages in this formation are of LMS standard design, including an almost brand new Stanier pattern dining car, three from the rear. This was Third Class No.101 (the only one of its kind in Scotland at the time) which precisely identifies the train as the 1935 version of the 11.55am from Perth - the rostered circuit for this car which worked from Glasgow to Aviemore only.

The through coaches seem mostly to be at the front (vehicles two and three are LMS standard corridor brake composites) but there is no sign of the LNER stock from Edinburgh which might have been expected - again see Table I. It is, of course, possible that the train was being worked in more than one part (not unusual at busy times) and that there were alterations in 1936, on which Table I is based; but the picture clearly shows the nature of some of the changes which were beginning to appear during the mid-1930s. (Author's collection)

At more important locations, the many and various wagons from these local freights would be reorganised by destination to form longer-distance trains. Likewise, the in-coming longer distance trains would be broken up to form the delivery part of

the same local operations. In LMS days, these longer distance trains were generally known as Express or Through freights, depending mainly on the number of intermediate stops and/or the nature of the wagons themselves.

The 'Through Freight' was defined simply as "running not less than 15 miles without stopping" and could convey any sort of wagon, no matter how primitive. Next in ascending order were the 'Express Freights' which usually ran further and faster between stops and had to consist solely of wagons with more modern axleboxes - ie lubricated with oil (always fluid) not grease (which relied on axle friction to liquify the semi-solid lubricant). Neither category needed to contain vehicles with an automatic brake operated by the locomotive; but an express freight could convey such wagons if present (they were called 'fitted' vehicles) and if present, they were marshalled at the front of the train, thus putting more braking power at the driver's disposal. If there were at least four fitted wagons, such trains were allowed to proceed at even higher speed - generally referred to as 'Maltese Freights' because of the Maltese Cross symbol which identified them in the working timetables.

There were higher categories of express freight trains which had a larger proportion of fitted vehicles and there were even some trains (very few) which ran 'fully fitted'. There were also dedicated 'Mineral' trains defined by the LMS which rested at a point somewhere between ordinary and through freights; but these more specialised categories were never regularly seen on the Highland lines in LMS days as far as is known..... Also, as mentioned earlier in the chapter, a fair quantity of what can only be seen as 'goods' traffic was carried in non-passenger coaching stock (NPCS) attached to scheduled passenger trains.

These latter operations were not classified as freight, of course, and on many busy LMS main lines would regularly run as dedicated NPCS workings, often but not always accurately described as 'Parcels Trains' and travelling at full passenger train speed. As far as can be determined, there were no 100% dedicated 'parcels' trains in the regular Highland schedules,

This view at Boat of Garten indicates that the LMS was not the only company to import 'foreign' carriage stock after the grouping. This was the furthest point south reached by the independent GNSR Speyside line and LNER trains terminated there, using the Highland's station facilities. This picture of the carriage siding shows what was probably a typical 'scratch' set, consisting of ex-North Eastern, GNSR and Great Central stock respectively. The former GNSR line entered from the right in the distance but the date is not known.　　　(The late Gavin Wilson)

though there were a few 'as required' exceptions from time to time. Two such examples are listed as annotations to the 1939 working timetables when a dedicated newspaper train ran on Sunday mornings at 06.09 from Perth to Inverness (and then onwards to Lairg, arriving at 11.20), together with the provision of a qualified path for a horsebox special (SX if required) leaving Perth for Aviemore at 4.20pm. But despite the relative lack of exclusively NPCS workings, the presence of these more versatile vehicles was always important on the Highland lines as many pictures of them attached to passenger workings, often in quantity, bear ample witness. Indeed, this kind of evidence suggests that the proportion of such stock added to Highland passenger trains was higher than normally found elsewhere, probably because of a high volume of parcels traffic to outlying parts, albeit not sufficient to warrant dedicated workings.

Fortunately, for the purpose of analysis, freight timetables were rarely as complex as their passenger equivalent, probably because of the separation of categories as mentioned above and it is to this which I now turn, reminding readers of the caveat entered at the start of the chapter regarding the limitations of using but one sample year.

The combination of 'Crab' plus Class 5 was not unknown, but neither was it very common, especially as late as July 1939 when this view was taken at Slochd summit. But two engines would certainly be needed on this formation of at least thirteen carriages. The train is one of the rare Sunday only workings (4.10pm from Inverness: Table I) and the locomotives are Nos.2808 and 5151. Carriage types cannot easily be identified, save for the ex-MR 'strengthener' at the front of the train, but most of them are quite modern, including a fair number of flush sided Stanier types.

(Peter Tatlow Collection)

Freight Services: Perth and Inverness

The booked freight services on the principal Highland main line in 1929 are given at Table V and one's first reaction, given the remote nature of much of the hinterland, is that there were quite a lot of them. During most days of the week there were eleven services along the whole length of the line (six north and five south) plus one extra on Monday in the northbound direction, all taking the Carr Bridge route. Most of them ran at the same time all week (for exceptions see Table) and it is interesting to note that the northbound services were somewhat more complex than those going south. For example, the 16.05 through freight ex-Perth on Saturdays seems to have replaced the two late evening express freights which ran during the rest of the week; while another, the 04.25 ex-Perth, ran as an ordinary 'all stations' stopping freight for which there was no southbound equivalent. It is also worth noting that almost all the rest of 'full route' trains - and all those southbound save the 01.40 on Mondays and Fridays - ran as 'Maltese' freights (above), thus achieving some degree of speedier transit.

TABLE V: FREIGHT SERVICES PERTH-INVERNESS - AUTUMN 1929

Monday-Saturday, save where noted - no Sunday services. Arrival times quoted are those at the final destination given in the 'Details' column. The table uses the 24 hour clock in line with modern custom

NORTHBOUND

Time	Details
00.25(MX)	**Perth-Forres.** Arrived 06.59. Express Freight, running under 'Maltese Cross' rules - see text.
00.40(MO)	**Perth-Inverness via Carr Bridge.** Arrived 06.55. Express 'Maltese Cross' Freight
01.00(MO)	**Perth-Forres.** Arrived 06.59. Express 'Maltese Cross' Freight
01.55	**Perth-Inverness, via Carr Bridge.** Arrived 08.30. Through Freight, arriving 10 minutes later(MX) until 12th October
06.45	**Aviemore-Forres.** Arrived 09.21. Ordinary Freight
04.25	**Perth-Inverness via Carr Bridge.** Arrived 11.23. Ordinary Freight from 14th October
12.20(SX)	**Aviemore-Inverness via Carr Bridge.** Arrived 15.05. Ordinary Freight
08.00	**Perth-Forres.** Arrived 15.05. Express Freight
09.40	**Perth-Inverness via Carr Bridge.** Arrived 17.35. Express 'Maltese Cross' Freight until 12th October
10.20	**Perth-Aviemore.** Arrived 16.55. Through Freight,
17.55(SO)	**Aviemore-Boat of Garten.** Arrived 18.15. Ordinary Freight
19.25(SX)	**Aviemore-Boat of Garten.** Arrived 19.45. Ordinary Freight
14.25	**Perth-Inverness via Carr Bridge.** Arrived 22.15. Through Freight
16.05(SO)	**Perth-Inverness via Carr Bridge.** Arrived 23.30. Through Freight
17.15(MO)	**Perth-Aviemore.** Arrived 22.50. Through Freight
19.15(MX)	**Perth-Aviemore.** Arrived midnight. Through freight
21.25(SX)	**Perth-Inverness via Carr Bridge.** Arrived 04.24. Express 'Maltese Cross' Freight
23.25(SX)	**Perth-Inverness via Carr Bridge.** Arrived 06.35. Express 'Maltese Cross' Freight

SOUTHBOUND

Time	Details
00.15(MX)	**Inverness-Perth via Carr Bridge.** Arrived 07.05. Express 'Maltese Cross' Freight
00.35(MO)	**Inverness-Perth via Carr Bridge.** Arrived 07.05. Express 'Maltese Cross' Freight
01.40(MFX)	**Inverness-Perth via Carr Bridge.** Arrived 08.04. Express 'Maltese Cross' Freight
01.40(MFO)	**Inverness-Perth via Carr Bridge.** Arrived 09.40. Through Freight
10.20	**Aviemore-Perth.** Arrived 16.08. Ordinary Freight from 2nd October
10.50(SX)	**Aviemore-Perth.** Arrived 17.07. Ordinary Freight until 1st October
10.50(SO)	**Aviemore-Perth.** Arrived 17.37. Ordinary Freight until 28th September
08.45(SX)	**Inverness-Aviemore via Carr Bridge.** Arrived 11.35. Ordinary Freight
11.00	**Forres-Aviemore.** Arrived 13.30. Ordinary Freight
11.50	**Forres-Perth.** Arrived 18.20. Express 'Maltese Cross' Freight
12.20	**Inverness-Perth via Carr Bridge.** Arrived 18.55. Express 'Maltese Cross' Freight
17.35	**Forres-Perth.** Arrived 22.59. Express 'Maltese Cross' Freight
17.25	**Inverness-Perth via Carr Bridge.** Arrived 23.27. Express 'Maltese Cross' Freight
19.20(SO)	**Boat of Garten-Perth.** Arrived 00.27. Express Freight
20.45(SX)	**Boat of Garten-Perth.** Arrived 01.02. Express Freight
20.45(SX)	**Inverness-Perth via Carr Bridge.** Arrived 03.08. Express 'Maltese Cross' Freight

These two superb front and rear views were taken at Inverness in 1930 and show LMS 2-6-0 No.13105 and 'Castle' Class 4-6-0 No.14677 Dunrobin Castle backing onto a train prior to a double-headed southbound departure. Both of them feature the characteristic wooden planked outer platform surfaces at that time, while the first picture also shows some details of No.17957, one of the Cumming 4-6-0 'Clan Goods' as they were sometimes called. The rear view shows some typical Highland signals - the left hand shunting arm in the 'off' position probably applying to the aforementioned Cumming 4-6-0 on the adjoining track. Note that although both the 2-6-0 and 'Castle' are known to have carried lined black livery, the red lining has failed to register at all.

(Gordon Coltas - 2)

Bottom: This undated departure from Inverness shows what is almost certainly the 4.15pm southbound working from mid-August to late September only (16.15 - Table I). Jones 4-4-0 No.14391 Loch Shin is piloting an unidentified 'Castle' 4-6-0 from the 6ft driving wheel series and the fact that both engines are of HR origin and that some carriages are rather elderly lends support to the supposition that this was an extra train run at peak periods only. The formation of the train, all gangwayed types and listed back from the engines, was LMS full brake; LMS corridor composite; LMS third class sleeping car; ex-WCJS clerestory first class sleeping car; LNER brake third; LNER composite sleeping car; LNER first class sleeping car. The writer cannot resist the thought that this is a nice prototype train for dedicated modellers..... (Peter Tatlow Collection)

47

This July 1947 view, taken on the northbound platforms at Inverness, shows just how much the nature of trains for the Far North line had changed by the end of the LMS period. It is but the humble 8.45am local to Tain (post-war equivalent of the 9.20am listed at Table III) but such as can be seen of the train is composed wholly of modern Stanier corridor stock. The engine is 4-6-0 No.17953, one of the Cumming 'Clan Goods' and a type increasingly associated with workings north of Inverness as the LMS period progressed. (John Edgington)

In this view, the mid-day Tain-Inverness local (12.40pm in 1936 - Table III) is seen leaving Tain on 4th August 1945: the return working of the train seen leaving Inverness some two years later in the previous view. It appears to be composed mostly of gangwayed stock, albeit not so modern - the leading corridor third is ex-LNWR and there is only one Stanier type in the formation. The engine in charge is an ex-Caledonian 'import' in the shape of Dunalastair II 4-4-0 No.14332, a type not as often associated with the Highland lines as later CR 4-4-0 designs. This particular locomotive was scrapped in 1946. (Ian Wright, courtesy Peter Tatlow)

The reason for the slight operational difference between the two directions is not entirely clear, but may, perhaps, be indicative of local operating differences north and south of Aviemore, almost certainly to serve the specific needs of the local traders, especially between Aviemore and Forres. What is also clear is that the bulk of the intermediate southbound services were destined for Perth, whereas those in the opposite direction were somewhat more varied in terms of destination.

In either direction, a broad trend can be observed: most of the full distance trains ran either overnight or fairly late in the evening, whereas the intermediate services operated mostly during the daylight hours. This is logical enough and strongly hints at the latter being used mainly to concentrate outward bound wagons at the larger centres from which ran the longer distance services - and vice-versa for inward bound traffic, of course. This should not be taken to imply that all traffic was thus concentrated, for at the same time, almost all the express and through freight workings were scheduled to stop at many of the intermediate locations. Sometimes this was to allow the faster passenger services to overtake, but it is highly likely that wagons carrying higher priority traffic would often be attached or detached to these trains to save excess wagon movement.

It is also worth mentioning that the overnight nature of much of the long distance freight working was not confined to the Highland Section - it was characteristic of the whole of the British railway network at the time and had two advantages. In the first place, it allowed earlier delivery at destination and secondly, it allowed better use to be made of the system at a time of day when passenger trains were all but absent. This was especially valid on the Highland with its long mileage of single track, but one cannot escape the thought that many of our present road congestion problems might be alleviated to a very considerable extent if long distance trunk freight haulage could mostly be confined to the c.7pm-7am period, just as the railways used to do........

continued on page 53

During the repair and overhaul of the turntable at the Kyle of Lochalsh in 1946, Fairburn 2-6-4Ts (which had arrived on the Highland section by then - see Chapter 5) were drafted into the Inverness area to compensate for lack of turning facilities at The Kyle. It will occasion no surprise to know that the late Henry Casserley was present to record some of this unusual activity, believed to be the only instance of tank locomotives working the full length of this route. They are thought to have been confined to passenger workings (slower goods trains could, of course, be operated tender first) and this is No.2216 with a very modestly sized Kyle train at Muir of Ord in April 1946 - service unknown. A horsebox is at the front and the train is a typical late-LMS three-coach corridor set: two brake thirds flanking a composite, the latter apearing to be of LNWR origin in this case.

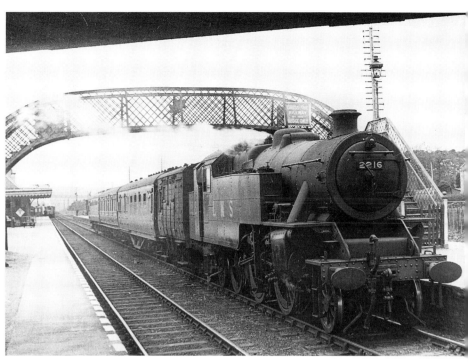

High activity at Achnashellach in June 1927, typifying the characteristic operation at passing places on single track lines at the time: frantic action for a short period followed by long intervals of calm contemplation. The high level view prevents the exact identification of vehicle types, but no two seem to be alike and both trains appear to be 'mixed' - see main text. The approaching engine is Jones 'Skye Bogie' 4-4-0 No.14283 and there is no reason to suppose that the one going the opposite way is not of the same type.

(The late H.C.Casserley)

Apart from a bit of LMS stock repainting, this 21st May 1926 view of the rail entry to Kyle of Lochalsh is hardly any different from that which would have been seen in Highland days. The anonymous photographer recorded the train (in charge of 'Skye Bogie' No.14284) as being the 10.20am ex-Inverness, but it is clearly a mixed train, only four carriages before coming to the freight stock. By 1936, this departure, now 10.15am from Inverness, was THE LEWISMAN (Table III) and would not not have had the sort of formation seen in this view. The angle of shadow, given the May date, is such as to suggest late afternoon or early in the evening and it is felt that the train is actually the late afternoon mixed train departure from Dingwall, again see Table III. (The late Gavin Wilson Collection)

Drummond 4-6-0 Ballindalloch Castle (LMS No.14676) enters The Mound with a train for Wick on 19th May 1928, probably the mid-morning 'almost all stations' service. The roof of the one carriage clearly visible on the Dornoch branch train (left) clearly indicates the difference in levels of the two lines as the main line continues its climb from this junction. (The late H.C.Casserley)

The writer has been unable to find any suitable pictures of main line trains at Wick itself during LMS days. Therefore, although the branch from Wick to Lybster will be covered in more detail in Chapter 4, this view of the branch train entering Wick will also have to stand duty at this point. It shows one of the so-called 'Yankee' 4-4-0Ts, LMS No.15013, in charge of a typical short mixed train. Perhaps the most interesting point to note is that although the locomotive is already repainted in LMS red, the sole passenger-carrying carriage, a six-wheel composite of Lancashire and Yorkshire Railway origin, is still bearing LYR colours.

(Peter Tatlow Collection)

This view of an eastbound train leaving Inverness for the Keith line c.1930 is of particular interest in showing a rather unusual mixture of both LMS and LNER stock. The carriages, all gangwayed, are marshalled with two LNER examples at the front, for what at first may seem to be an ex-Midland clerestory type immediately behind the locomotive is actually a 48ft corridor brake composite of Midland and North British Joint Stock origin, many of which were transferred to sole LNER ownership when the ex-M&NB Stock was split between the LMS and LNER in 1928. The second carriage is an ex-NBR corridor third and the rest of the train is LMS, of which a standard 60ft brake composite and 57ft ex-LNWR third are behind the ex-NBR coach. The locomotive itself is one of the three 6ft driving wheel Drummond 'Castle' Class 4-6-0s No.14692 Darnaway Castle.

(Peter Tatlow Collection)

This undated but probably c.1931-2 view shows a Jones 'Loch' Class 4-4-0 (believed to be No.14394 Loch Ashie, still with original boiler and chimney) arriving at Inverness with a train of LNER coaches from Aberdeen. As with contemporary LMS trains, the origins of the stock are many and various, in this case including identifiable ex-GNSR, GNR (ECJS?) and NER types at the front.

(Peter Tatlow Collection)

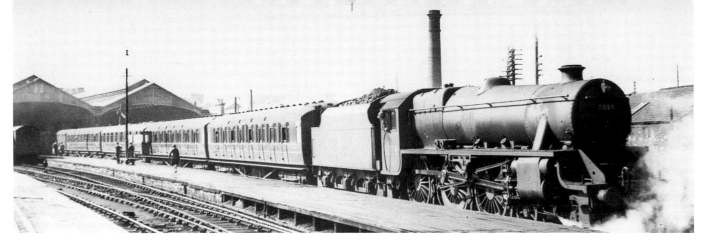

By 1939, Class 5 4-6-0s were also rostered to the Keith line and this picture shows No.5018 at Inverness with what will be the 1.00pm to Keith, conveying through carriages which formed the only dining car service between Inverness and Aberdeen. The portion of the train seen in the picture (detached at Elgin and worked from there by the LNER) was composed of LNER stock and the dining car appears to be the third vehicle, any LMS carriages for Keith being out of sight on the left. Note that the locomotive carries stopping passenger headlamps, an indication of the fact that on LMS metals (see Table IV), it was almost an all stations local. (Peter Tatlow Collection)

Interchange at Gollanfield Junction on 21st May 1931. On the right, Drummond 'Small Ben' 4-4-0 No.14398 Ben Alder heads the Fort George branch train, already signalled to depart, while arriving on the main line, an unidentified stopping service is in charge of 'River' Class 4-6-0 No.14759. This was a locomotive type designed for the Highland, but sold to the Caledonian pre-1923, only to be re-imported by the LMS after the grouping - see also Chapter 5.

(The late H.C.Casserley)

Taken at Forres in the early 1930s, this picture shows Drummond 'Small Ben' 4-4-0 No.14404 Ben Clebrig in charge of a two-coach local train. The working is not specified but the train is typical: ex-LYR corridor brake third leading plus ex-CR semi-corridor composite - ie with side corridor access to central lavatories but no end gangways to adjacent vehicles.

(Michael Blakemore Collection)

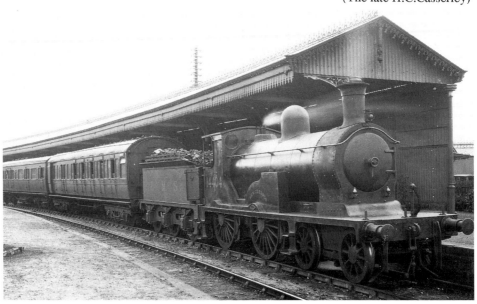

This July 1929 picture shows one of the last duties of 'Strath' Class 'Crewe-type' 4-4-0 No.14275 Glentruim, which was withdrawn in 1930. Taken leaving Orbliston Junction, the train is stated to be the 1.50pm 'all stations' service from Keith to Forres which, if the anonymous photographer was correct, was probably the precursor of the 13.45 Keith-Inverness in 1936 quoted at Table IV. The carriages are the usual random mixture of types and the trailing brake (ahead of the final goods van) could well be of G&SWR origin. The perceptive traveller would almost certainly opt for the Midland corridor third brake at the front! (M.Blakemore Collection)

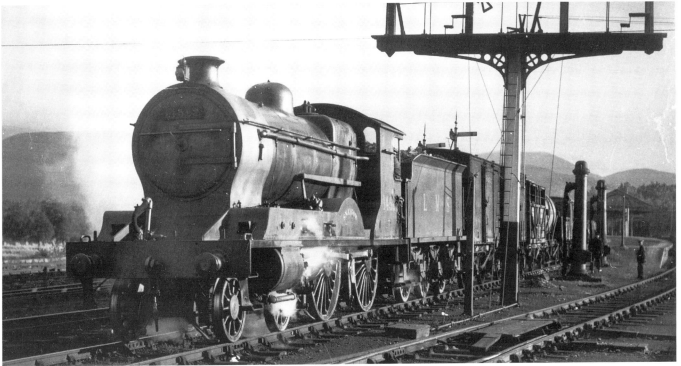

'Working' pictures in LMS days of the Cumming 4-4-0s, Snaigow and Durn are somewhat rare, but this view shows the former, No.14522, on duty at Aviemore right at the end of its life in 1936. The headlamp does not denote a stopping passenger train - it is the mandatory light carried when on the sort of shunting duty to which the engine seems now to have been relegated, reinforced by the evidence of the shunting signal in the 'off' position. Note also, the double water columns to the right of the signal post. This was a typical Highland feature which, on the many double-headed trains operated on the line during both Highland and LMS days, allowed both locomotives to take on water simultaneously. (Author's collection)

Freight Services: North of Inverness

North of Inverness, the pattern of freight traffic was rather different and is summarised at Table VI. Here, collection and distribution using ordinary freight trains was more dominant and it will be noted that only two trains ran the full length of the Far North line daily in each direction. Neither of them merited 'express' category, they stopped at many places and took the best part of twelve hours to make the full 161 mile journey between Inverness and Wick.

TABLE VI: FREIGHT SERVICES, INVERNESS-KYLE OF LOCHALSH & THE FAR NORTH - AUTUMN 1929

Monday-Saturday, save where noted - no Sunday services. Arrival times quoted are those at the final destination given in the 'Details' column. The table uses the 24 hour clock in line with modern custom

NORTHBOUND

Time	Details
04.10	**Helmsdale-Wick.** Arrived 08.00. Ordinary Freight
05.50(TThSO)	**Inverness-Wick.** Arrived 16.55. Through Freight
07.35	**Inverness-Helmsdale.** Arrived 15.40. Ordinary Freight
08.56	**Dingwall-Kyle of Lochalsh.** Arrived 12.55. Ordinary Freight
08.00	**Inverness-Dingwall.** Arrived 10.38. Ordinary Freight
11.55	**Dingwall-Achterneed.** Arrived 12.10. Ordinary Freight, then to Raven's Rock (arr 12.20)
13.20(TThSO)	**Tain-Bonar Bridge.** Arrived 14.25. Ordinary Freight, noted as leaving the Glenmorangie siding at 13.35
11.30(SX)	**Inverness-Wick.** Arrived 23.35. Through Freight
11.30(SO)	**Inverness-Helmsdale.** Arrived 18.53. Through Freight
15.50	**Inverness-Tain.** Arrived 21.45. Ordinary Freight

SOUTHBOUND

Time	Details
00.05	**Wick-Inverness.** Arrived 11.35. Through Freight
09.10	**Tain-Inverness.** Arrived 15.35. Ordinary Freight
12.46	**Achterneed-Dingwall.** Arrived 13.08. Ordinary Freight
07.45	**Helmsdale-Inverness.** Arrived 15.50. Through Freight
15.25(TThSO)	**Bonar Bridge-Tain.** Arrived 16.30. Ordinary Freight, noted as leaving the Glenmorangie siding at 16.25
11.45(WFO)	**Kyle of Lochalsh-Dingwall.** Arrived 15.25. Ordinary Freight
09.00(MWFO)	**Wick-Inverness.** Arrived 20.25. Through Freight
16.40	**Tain-Inverness.** Arrived 22.05. Ordinary Freight

That said, there was clearly a fair amount of intermediate traffic, so some degree of concentration at larger locations must have taken place; and there were also a few shorter runs too. Of these we may perhaps single out the thrice weekly Tain-Bonar Bridge operation whose annotation seems to give the main reason, needing no form of additional explanation to lovers of 'The Malt' - sic! It is also worth mentioning that with one early morning exception in both directions, all scheduled freight trains on the Far North line were timed to arrive at destination after mid-day - no doubt to connect with overnight services as and where appropiate

On the Kyle line, freight trains operated exclusively from Dingwall, at which point vehicles to or from the Kyle route would either be detached from or attached to trains serving the Far North line. The fact that there was only one scheduled daily working along the whole of the route to Kyle of Lochalsh from Dingwall (at 08.56) is in part explained by the presence of the daily mixed train in both directions already considered earlier in the chapter and included at Table III. But note that there was no balancing daily working in the opposite direction to the 08.56 down train. Instead, there was a twice weekly train at 11.45 which, when it ran, crossed the daily down freight at Strome Ferry. This may have reflected some form of non-daily local traffic variation (livestock, perhaps?) which the timetable does not identify.

There was also a daily lunch time shuttle between Dingwall and Achterneed, extended to Raven's Rock Quarry, the latter being operated by the local authorities for the extraction of road stone. This useful source of railway revenue was opened in early LMS days and at its peak produced 120 tons per day; but it had ceased operations by June 1939.

Freight Services: Inverness and Keith

Compared with the complications elsewhere, freight working on this section of the Highland lines was relatively simple and is summarised at Table VII. The vast majority of trains were, in effect, all stations local operations, presumably assembling or delivering wagons en-route to or received from locations of a more distant nature. Indeed, there was only one train per day along the whole route, running eastbound only from Inverness at 11.40. No reason can be adduced why no westbound train of similar type was operated from Keith.

However, what the table does reveal is that quite a number of differently identified 'local' routes were served by their own dedicated trains. To a large extent, but not exclusively, these services concentrated mostly on Forres, which must have been an interesting place in those days. Much of this traffic was related to the LMS main line south via Dava, of course, but as far as the LMS was concerned, Forres may well also have been the most profitable point from which to receive or distribute traffic whose revenue receipts had to be shared with the LNER - we shall probably never know at this distance in time......

TABLE VII: FREIGHT SERVICES, INVERNESS-KEITH - AUTUMN 1929

Monday-Saturday, save where noted - no Sunday services. Arrival times quoted are those at the final destination given in the 'details' column. The table uses the 24 hour clock in line with modern custom

EASTBOUND

Time	Details
09.10	**Forres-Elgin.** Arrived 10.35. Ordinary Freight
11.10(MTX)	**Mulben-Keith.** Arrived 11.20. Ordinary Freight *
11.20	**Inverness-Gollanfield Jct.** Arrived 12.16. Ordinary Freight
11.40	**Inverness-Keith.** Arrived 16.40. Through Freight
14.30	**Nairn-Forres.** Arrived 15.40. Ordinary Freight
16.30	**Inverness-Forres.** Arrived 18.40. Ordinary Freight
18.55(MTO)	**Tauchers-Keith.** Arrived 19.05. Ordinary Freight

WESTBOUND

Time	Details
07.10	**Forres-Inverness.** Arrived 09.35. Ordinary Freight
05.10	**Keith-Forres.** Arrived 08.10. Ordinary Freight
08.25	**Forres-Inverness.** Arrived 09.55. Through Freight
10.30(MTX)	**Keith-Mulben.** Arrived 11.05. Ordinary Freight *
11.50	**Forres-Nairn.** Arrived 12.20. Ordinary Freight
14.45	**Elgin-Forres.** Arrived 15.50. Ordinary Freight
16.15(FO)	**Elgin-Forres.** Arrived 17.02. Ordinary Freight *
18.30(MTO)	**Keith-Tauchers.** Arrived 18.40. Ordinary Freight
20.20(MTX)	**Forres-Inverness.** Arrived 22.20. Ordinary Freight

* These trains ran when required

Freight Services: Local shunting

It will be apparent from the above summaries that the marshalling and re-marshalling of freight trains at the more important locations was a vital part of the whole operation. For the most part, shunting at intermediate locations along the line was carried out by the train engine itself, but once wagons had arrived in the main marshalling yards at what might be perhaps be called 'major distribution points', this no longer sufficed, additional locomotive power being essential for this far more complex and time-consuming operation. In consequence, the working freight timetables regularly included details of the shunting engines needed for this task.

Those provided for the Highland section were duly recorded and the 1929 situation is summarised below. There is no good reason to suppose that things changed very much in principle during most of the LMS era, so the nature of the jobs can be taken as reasonably typical of a much longer period and they are listed alphabetically by location. It should also be noted that not all these additional locomotive duties were confined to shunting in the immediately local goods yards and that the duties do not specify the engine type.........

Aviemore: At this location three duties were specified. No.1 was from 04.00 to to 12.00 mid-day and was unique in being almost entirely concerned with assisting the trains to Slochd Summit as required, this being a reflection of the fact that all the principal freight trains from the south took this route - see earlier in the chapter. Duties No.2 (07.00-15.00) and No.3 (13.00-21.00) were routine shunting jobs at and around the station, both passenger and freight - but note the overlap between these two duties from 13.00-15.00.

Dingwall: One dedicated shunting roster only was specified (between 13.30 and 21.30), confined solely to goods traffic. This was the critical period for such activity - see earlier in this chapter.

Forres: As stated earlier in the chapter, not least in connection with the Inverness and Keith services, Forres was a pivotal point and had two dedicated 'freight only' jobs lasting for most of the day. Forming a continuous operation from 05.15 onwards, Crew No.1 booked on at that time and worked until 13.05 when they were relieved by Crew No.2 who booked on at 12.55, finally booking off when 'work is completed', to use the somewhat euphemistic term quoted in the LMS book.....

Inverness: Here, as might be expected, the situation was far more complex. Six goods rosters were specified, along with a bit of topping up by way of a half share of a (notional) passenger job, listed at the end of the following summary, but whose other duties are unknown to this writer. From them, it is clear that the goods yard was being shunted 24 hours per day and at least five locomotives were involved, Nos.1-3 being performed by the same engine:

No.1: 00.15-08.00. Shunts Inverness goods yard relieving No.3 at 00.30

No.2: 08.00-15.45. Shunts Inverness goods yard relieving No.1. Engine to sheds for servicing at 15.45

No.3: 16.45-00.30, engine off shed at 17.30 to shunt Inverness goods yard and relieved by No.1 at 00.30

No.4: 08.15 (off shed at 09.00) for Inverness Harbour branch - returned to shed at 16.00

No.5: 07.15 (off shed at 08.00) for Carriage and Wagon workshop shunting duty - returned to shed at 15.00

No.6: 05.25 (off shed at 06.00) - Milburn goods sidings duty. Engine returned to shed at 13.00

No.7: 16.00-18.00. Shunts Inverness goods yard, worked by Passenger Engine turn No.10, relieving the rostered locomotive for duties 1-3 while the latter was 'on shed'.

Footnote: Passenger and freight workings on the various ex-HR branch lines are considered separately in Chapter 4. **LMS**

Much freight activity at Inverness in August 1939. In the foreground, Drummond 0-6-0 No.17698, one of the so-called 'Barneys', sets off in the Forres direction with an express freight, possibly the 1939 version of the 11.40am through freight of 1929 (Table VII), while LMS Class 3F 0-6-0T No.7541 is busy shunting in the background. Behind the tender of 17698, an unidentified Class 5 4-6-0 is seen tackling the start of the ascent to Slochd Summit and will soon bear right to pass over the foreground route. (Peter Tatlow Collection)

Livestock working was a strong feature of Highland freight train activity, extra trains often being needed at the seasonal 'peaks' of stock movement between the highland and lowland areas. In this busy scene at Inverness c.1939, both cattle and sheep are being put into stock pens prior to being loaded into livestock wagons, the vital thing being that the animals should not be kept in the stock pens for too long before loading and that the vehicles, once loaded, should be on their way as soon as possible.
(Peter Tatlow Collection)

Freight was handled on both sides of the central platform at Kyle of Lochalsh and this early view shows the southern half. Dominant in the left foreground are barrels of fish oil loaded into open wagons, on the nearest of which is a chalked inscription, mostly illegible but including a 26th June date which could be either 1913 or 1923. Given the intervention of war, it is very unlikely that much would have changed between the two dates, even if the picture is from the earlier time.
(Author's collection)

These almost identical views of the northern half of the railway pier at Kyle of Lochalsh are separated by the best part of 20 years yet show many similarities. In the earlier view, red-painted 'Skye Bogie' 4-4-0 No.14279 is preparing outward bound freight traffic in June 1927, while in the second, an unidentified 'Clan Goods' 4-6-0 is doing much the same sort of job in late LMS days. Both engines are carrying 'stopping freight' headlamp code and likely to have been preparing the mid-day departure for Dingwall. In the background to the first picture, a typically varied clutch of passenger carriages can be seen at the platform (ex-LYR; ex-MR; ex-HR) plus an ex-MR full brake beyond. (The late H.C.Casserley, Author's collection)

This interesting view shows a pair of 'imported' 0-6-0s on southbound freight duty at Blair Atholl in the later 1930s. The train carries 'Through Freight' headlamps, which makes it hard to identify from the working timetable, but the number of covered vans at the head of the train is worthy of note and could indicate that the train had a 'fitted head' despite the headcode - see text. The train engine is an unidentified LMS Class 4F 0-6-0, almost certainly one of the seven sent to Perth in the 1920s - see Chapter 5 - but the leading locomotive is an ex-CR Pickersgill '300 Class' 0-6-0 No.17663, carrying a Perth shed plate and probably requisitioned at short notice to work the Highland line on this day.

(The late Gavin Wilson Collection)

A southbound ordinary freight in charge of an unidentified Drummond 'Barney' 0-6-0 (possibly No.17693) 'gets the road' at Tain in August 1939. Note the driver checking back down the train and the relatively high proportion of covered van traffic.   (Peter Tatlow Collection)

A typical mixture of non-passenger coaching stock (LMS full brake and parcels van) and orthodox freight vehicles (covered van and cattle wagon) is seen here being shunted at Strathcarron at the start of the BR period: June 1948. The locomotive, 'Clan Goods' 4-6-0 No.17951 is heading in the Kyle direction and carries through freight headlamps, but the precise working is not known.

(Author's collection)

4

The Highland Branch Lines

AT THE END OF ITS LIFE, The Highland Railway owned no fewer than ten branch lines, all but one being of conventional 'Junction to Terminus' type. Paradoxically it was the one exception (Keith to Portessie) which was the first partial casualty, being closed to passengers in 1915; but they all came into LMS ownership. Although the LMS eventually closed about half the rest to passengers, all but two of them carried freight traffic until BR days, the overall situation down to 1948 being summarised in Table VIII. For the sake of completeness, this table also includes the pre-1923 closure details.

TABLE VIII: HIGHLAND BRANCH LINES IN LMS DAYS

Ballinluig Junction to Aberfeldy: 8.75 miles - remained open
Muir of Ord to Fortrose: 13.5 miles - remained open
Fodderty Junction to Strathpeffer: 2.5 miles - closed to passengers in 1946
The Mound to Dornoch: 7.75 miles - remained open
Georgemas Junction to Thurso: 6.75 miles - remained open
Wick to Lybster: 13.75 miles - closed completely in 1944
Gollanfield Jct to Fort George: 1.5 miles - closed to passengers in 1943
Alves to Hopeman: 7.5 miles - closed to passengers 1931
Orbliston Junction to Fochabers: 3 miles - closed to passengers in 1931
Keith to Portessie: 13.75 miles - closed to passengers 1915: Portessie to Buckie closed completely in 1944

From this summary, it will be appreciated that apart from the pre-group closure to passengers of the Keith-Portessie route and the early cessation of passenger traffic to Hopeman and Fochabers, the LMS kept the rest of the branches fully active for all traffic until well into the war years. Furthermore, from the frequency of services which the LMS usually offered along many of these lines during its time at the helm, the strong impression is gained that a truly determined effort was made throughout the whole grouping period to maintain as high a standard of service as possible on what must have been, at best, somewhat marginal routes. This was also, of course, the time when local bus services were beginning to expand and, as will be seen, passenger services on some of the Highland branches were victims of the greater flexibility

Ballinluig, the junction for the Aberfeldy branch looking towards Perth - date unknown but the locomotive in the distance is one of the LMS standard Class 4F 0-6-0s sent to the area in the 1920s - see Chapter 5. The branch itself came into the station from the right behind the main building. (The late Gavin Wilson)

LMS period views of the Aberfeldy line seem to be rather rare. However, even though taken some ten years or more after the period of this book, this picture is wholly relevant in context since it shows the typical LMS approach to branch working on the Highland system in later years. Ex-Caledonian 0-4-4T No.55217 waits to depart from Ballinluig with a single corridor brake composite of modern LMS design (built in 1930 and given 'Stanier' windows and panelling c.1939). The use of modern brake composites as single vehicles on the branch lines was very common in LMS days. (Peter Tatlow Collection)

---

which this mode of operation offered, especially where the terrain was relatively easy for road transport.

In this chapter, the branches will be considered in the order listed at Table VIII. This relates directly to the three main routes with which they were in connection and is offered in the sequence in which their respective main lines were covered in Chapter 2. As in that chapter, services are analysed mostly by reference to the 1929 (freight) and 1936 (passenger) situations whose characteristics, as already explained, seem reasonably typical of LMS practice over quite a long period of time. As with the main line services already considered, this review

should be taken only as typifying the general nature of LMS operations; there were undoubtedly slight variations over time.

The Aberfeldy Branch

This, the most southerly of the Highland branches, was the only such example south of Inverness and connected with the main line from Perth at Ballinluig. Authorised in 1854 as part of an earlier proposal which got as far as Dunkeld in 1856, the idea was floated well before the main line north of Dunkeld eventually received its own Act in 1861. However, in want of an extension north of Dunkeld until after the main line was opened in 1863, Aberfeldy was not finally reached until July 1865. It was an expensive line to build, there being 41 bridges along its less than nine mile length, and held the distinction of being the first new stretch of line to be opened after the adoption of the name Highland Railway (in June 1865) by the various companies which had amalgamated during that year. Balnaguard Halt between Ballinluig and Grantully was added by the LMS and opened in December 1935.

It survived well into BR days and during the LMS period it enjoyed a comprehensive service, being one of relatively few Highland branches not to be worked by 'one engine in steam'. In 1936, it had eight or nine daily passenger trains in each direction plus an extra one or two on Saturdays. There were

This undated but early LMS view shows an unidentified ex-CR 0-4-4T running round its train at Aberfeldy. The quality is not of the best but it shows the substantial nature of the station and its rarity value is of interest. A former Highland carriage in fully lined LMS livery, now LMS No.18843, is seen in the siding on the left. It was probably kept at Aberfeldy for strengthening purposes if so required.
(Peter Tatlow Collection)

also one or two through carriage workings from Perth - see Chapter 3 Table I. The regular departures from Aberfeldy ran from c.7.00am to 6.49pm, plus two extra evening services on Saturdays, the only significantly long interval being between 8.52am and 12.30pm. Services were not exactly balanced, for in the reverse direction there were nine trains per day between 7.40am and 9.05pm, plus one extra late on Saturday, the longest interval between them again being in the late morning between 10.25am and 1.05pm. It would seem from the actual times that at least one or two locomotives were based at Aberfeldy and it was from this end of the line that the daily services commenced.

Freight along the Aberfeldy branch was generally by way of authorising some of the regular passenger services to run as mixed trains. These ran four times per day in each direction during 1929 and this pattern seems to have continued. There were some qualified exceptions of which an interesting note states that the 3.55pm from Aberfeldy ran as a mixed train only when livestock was to be carried.

The Black Isle Branch

The line from Muir of Ord to Fortrose ran along that somewhat inaccessible region between the Cromarty and Beauly Firths, always known as the 'Black Isle'. It contains some fine farm land, while Fortrose itself is an ancient cathedral town which expanded into a small holiday resort. The line was originally intended to go to Rosemarkie and was opened to Fortrose in 1894, a distance of some 13.5 miles, but the further extension of just over two miles was never built. A study of the map will reveal that the route to Inverness from Fortrose is anything but direct, but without expensive bridge building across the Beauly Firth, hardly viable economically, the longer distance via Muir of Ord was the only practical solution.

The line remained open for passenger and freight during the whole LMS period, being one of many Highland branches to be worked by 'one engine in steam'. In consequence, services were of a 'balanced' nature and as with most branches, daily activities started at the terminus end. Four passenger trains ran in each direction during 1936, leaving Fortrose at 7.00am, 9.05am or 9.15am (depending on the day of the week), 1.15pm and 4.40pm and coming back at 7.55am, 10.05am, 3.25pm and 5.40pm. Some of these may well have run as 'mixed' from time to time, though the timetable was not annotated as such. There was also a daily pick-up freight train from Fortrose which was scheduled to run at 10.55am in 1929, returning at 12.15pm and clearly designed to interlock with passenger services, making use of the same locomotive. There is every reason to suppose that this basic pattern typified most of the LMS period.

That well known railway photographer, the late Henry Casserley, was on hand at Muir of Ord junction on 21st May 1928 to capture this nice little operating cameo. In the first picture, the Black Isle branch train has just arrived behind 'Skye Bogie' 4-4-0 No.14277 to connect with the southbound local approaching on the main line. The latter is double headed by a pair of 'Ben' Class 4-4-0s (one large and one small) with superheated 'Large Ben' No.14420 Ben a'Chait in the lead.

The second picture shows 14277 again (after turning) and about to proceed to Fortrose. From this and the previous view it can be seen that the train consists of three coaches, two ex-Highland brake thirds with central lookouts flanking a former LNWR arc roof carriage with lavatories - probably composite.

Later in LMS days, Inverness-based 'Small Ben' No.14409 Ben Alisky was in charge of the Black Isle branch train and is seen at the terminus with a very different sort of train: a leading six-compartment ex-WCJS corridor composite plus ex-LYR corridor brake third with inward tapering guard's van portion.
(Peter Tatlow Collection)

As with Aberfeldy, Fortrose seems to have escaped most LMS period photographers, but this c.1913 Highland Railway view shows a substantial station with typical gable-ended 'pavilions' flanking a central colonnade, albeit that the building is mostly made from corrugated sections rather than masonry. It is unlikely that it had changed much by LMS times. (The late Gavin Wilson Collection)

The Strathpeffer Branch

The Strathpeffer branch was one of many examples in Britain where early objection to the idea of a railway was to cause an important place to be by-passed, the original intention during the 1860s being that the proposed Dingwall and Skye Railway should go via Strathpeffer. Local landowners objected to the idea so firmly that sundry deviations were authorised in 1868, one of which resulted in a diversion to the north of the spa town via Raven's Rock Summit. It not only added four miles of unnecessary 1:50 gradient compared with the far easier and lower level route via Strathpeffer itself, but also deprived the town of a centrally located station on the main route west.

By the time changes in attitude had occured - ie the locals wanted a railway after all (sic!) - the revised route was already *fait accompli* and the only possible solution was to build a short line from Fodderty Junction, where the deviation turned sharp right on its climb to Raven's Rock. As a result, Strathpeffer did not get its own railway until 1885, at which time the station on the diverted main line which had carried its name (some 1.5 miles away at the top of a steep hill) was renamed Achterneed. The new branch kept to the lower ground, more or less along the alignment of the original planned route, terminating some 2.5 miles from the junction at an imposing station located centrally in the town. Fodderty junction itself was given emergency sidings during WWII to cater for the 'mine' trains making for the Kyle of Lochalsh.

The line was always worked from Dingwall, where trains made sundry connections, rather than from Fodderty Junction only and was given a very lavish service, including a few through carriages - see Chapter 3, Table III. In Summer 1936, there were no fewer than twelve trains each way daily between 8.11am and 9.15pm from Dingwall and between 8.30am and 9.35pm from the terminus. Some two thirds of these made

In the 1920s, the Strathpeffer branch saw an interesting variety of both locomotives and rolling stock - fortunately well photographed by contemporary observers. In this 1925 view, still carrying HR livery, 'Yankee' 4-4-0T No.101 (later LMS 15013) is seen at Dingwall with the branch train. The leading coaches are Highland long-wheelbase six-wheelers of different vintages, one all third (at the front), the other a composite and both already in LMS livery. Next comes an ex-Midland six wheel full brake followed by another ex-MR type, a 54ft corridor bogie brake composite. From all available evidence it seems that ex-MR stock was amongst the earliest to be imported into the Highlands.

(The late R.D.Stephen from the Author's collection)

By 1926, Stroudley 0-6-0T No.16118 was working some of the Strathpeffer trains and is seen here after arrival at the terminus. The train now consists of a Highland six-wheel luggage composite, followed by a Midland design arc-roof six-wheel third (conceivably ex-Midland Scottish Joint Stock via the G&SWR), a six wheel ex-MR clerestory full brake and, bringing up the rear, a 42ft bogie lavatory luggage composite of LNWR or WCJS origin, the only part of the train still bearing pre-1923 colours. Note the design similarity between Strathpeffer station (the most elaborate branch terminus on the HR) and that at Dingwall.

(The late R.D.Stephen from the Author's collection)

In May 1928, 'Small Ben' 4-4-0 No.14398 Ben Alder was on Strathpeffer branch duty, newly repainted in LMS lined black livery and 1928 style insignia. This locomotive was set aside for possible preservation between 1953 and 1967, only to be finally scrapped for the somewhat dubious reason that it was not quite in original Highland condition.... Lurking in the background is one of the relatively few LMS Sentinel steam railcars - see next view. (The late H.C.Casserley)

In 1926/7, the LMS purchased thirteen articulated steam railcars from Messrs Sentinel-Cammell, but never took to them quite as enthusiastically as did the LNER at much the same time, nor did it have as many. The LMS examples were smaller than those on the LNER and details of their workings are somewhat obscure. However, one or two were trialled on the Highland lines, No.4149 being seen at Strathpeffer in May 1928. It is not known how long it stayed on this duty but a similar railcar was noted in service at Perth in 1932.

(The late H.C.Casserley)

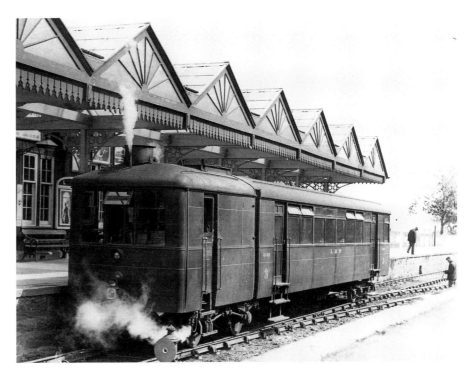

Red-painted 0-4-4T No.15052 prepares to leave Dornoch in May 1928. As can be seen, the station was close to the town centre and is obviously being patronised, though the open doors and drifting steam prevent the actual types of carriages from being determined. As far as can be judged, the engines on the Dornoch branch always worked chimney first towards The Mound.   (The late H.C.Casserley)

connections to and from locations served by Dingwall. In addition, the late morning train from Dingwall and the mid afternoon return service were scheduled as 'mixed'.

Unlike many places, Strathpeffer's role as a holiday resort and spa town was in large measure responsible for its regular service and these were, unsurprisingly, dramatically cut back during WWII when, as in WWI, many hotels and guest houses were taken over for use as hospitals and billets. Amongst them, the Spa Hotel (as a hospital) caught fire and was burned down during the second conflict. There being insufficient genuinely local traffic to keep things going immediately after the war, the line lost its passenger services completely in March 1946 and the freight traffic survived only three years after the demise of the LMS itself, the whole line closing in 1951. There can be little doubt that had Strathpeffer been on the Kyle line from the outset, it would still enjoy railway connection to this day.

The Dornoch Light Railway

This line resulted from the somewhat circuitous route taken by the Far North line after reaching Tain, where it headed well inland via Bonar Bridge to Lairg rather than face the expensive crossing of Dornoch Firth which a more direct route would have entailed. As a result, Dornoch (itself the county town of Sutherland) was left over seven miles from the railway, to which, for many years, it was connected only by road coach to the station at The Mound. In due course a connecting rail link was proposed in 1898 between Dornoch and The Mound and, once in existence, showed an amazing resilience during the whole of the LMS period. It was not opened until 1902 and was under LMS ownership longer than either its preceding or subsequent administrations. Built under light railway rules and always worked by the Highland until 1923, it kept its nominal independence until the grouping.

Although classified as a light railway, the Dornoch Branch, as it was often called, was built to almost main line standards and fully fenced, though the track itself was lighter than on the main line. Services were never very lavish in LMS days, even though some through carriages were operated - see Chapter 3, Table III. The basic offering was some four trains per day in each direction and worked by 'one engine in steam' which, like those on many other similar branches, was to start and finish its day at the terminus. In 1936, the first train left at 9.10am and the last arrived back at 7.20pm. The 9.10am from Dornoch

Taken on the same day, probably some time in the early 1930s, these views show the Dornoch branch train at both ends of the line in charge of 0-4-4T No.15054, now in LMS 1928 style lined black livery. In the first view, about to leave Dornoch, the main train consists of an ex-MR arc roof six-wheel third along with an ex-LNWR six-wheel composite (with third class half-compartment at the far end) and an ex-MR full brake. Beyond that is a former LNWR corridor bogie carriage which looks rather like a brake composite - almost certainly a through coach. At the other end of the line, 15054 has run round its train at The Mound, presumably shunted the through carriage for attachment to a southbound train on the main line and picked up some goods traffic to form a mixed train back to Dornoch. It is unlikely that this job is finished yet, there being no sign of the mandatory goods brake van at the rear of the train.

(Author's collection - 2)

ran as 'mixed', as did the second morning train in the opposite direction, the latter generally leaving The Mound between 11.00am and noon in LMS days.

It is one of the ironies of fate that although Dornoch somehow managed to retain its rail service until 1960, much against contemporary odds, the town itself might well have been re-connected to the railway network in our more modern era (1990s onwards) had the new A9 road bridge, across the narrowing of Dornoch Firth just north of Tain, been planned for both road and rail, thereby shortening the route to Wick and Thurso by both modes of transport. There was certainly some pressure to do just this, if only to reduce the advantage gained by bus operators, but genuine railway improvement was not too fashionable at that time......

The Thurso Branch

The Thurso Branch was an integral consequence of the somewhat complex development of the Far North line beyond Golspie. The original intention was to build a straightforward line from Wick to Thurso across fairly easy territory and this was duly authorised in 1866 as the Caithness Railway. This would later be extended by way of a link at some convenient intermediate point with a route south to Helmsdale. However, as things turned out, financial backing was difficult to get and nothing came of it for a few years and it was not until later that the Wick-Thurso line was built, now in conjunction with the main route south. The designated junction with the latter was at Georgemas and the whole railway was opened in 1874.

The nature of the junction was such that trains from Thurso joined the main line from the south so as to be able to proceed without reversal to Wick. This meant, in effect, that the Thurso to Georgemas stretch became a branch, involving reversal for any traffic proceeding to or from the south. Local services almost always proceeded to Wick, save for through carriages run in connection with main line line trains to and from the south. These were always attached or detached at Georgemas - and thus it remained throughout the LMS period.

The basic passenger service was just about adequate if not lavish and could, at times, get a bit complicated by the extra workings of through carriages along part of the route. Thus, in 1936 there were four through trains daily from Wick to Thurso between 8.45am and 6.45pm plus a late Saturday night only extra. In the reverse direction, only three through trains served the whole route, running at 10.05am, 5.05pm and 8.25pm, but

Georgemas Junction, July 1931, looking towards Thurso. The train itself extends round the curved part of the down platform and must therefore be presumed to have come from Thurso, not the main line. (The late H.C.Casserley)

a fourth service was available at 3.40pm by way of passengers changing from southbound through carriages at Georgemas and joining their northbound equivalents for Wick; but there was no Saturday only train in this direction. In addition, the 'Orcadian' offered a service between Georgemas and Wick at 12.32pm and the last daily through carriages for Thurso from the south left Georgemas at 8.55pm.

Freight traffic was equally light. The first train to Wick from Thurso ran as 'mixed' as did the 11.35am return. This was quite an operation for it picked up through carriages for Thurso at Georgemas. In early LMS days there was also a late evening freight at 9.15pm from Thurso which reversed at Georgemas, arriving back at Thurso at 10.15pm, though for what purpose and whether or not it lasted until later years (or made any useful connections for that matter) is not known.

All told, however, it must be said that LMS services along the Thurso line seemed to be very much a reflection of the limited economic potential of the area, no doubt combined with the adverse effect on the railway of the ever-growing bus services in a part of Scotland where the relatively easy nature of the terrain itself did not make road transport too difficult.

Thurso was another Highland terminus which seems to have been camera shy.... However, this undated, but probably immediately pre-LMS view of the station reveals it to have had a rather similar covered train shed to that found at Wick.

(Gavin Wilson Collection)

Interior view of the train shed at Wick in July 1931. That at Thurso is thought to have been similar, it having been built at much the same time.

(The late H.C.Casserley)

The Wick and Lybster Light Railway

Like the Dornoch Light Railway, this line too arose as a consequence of the Far North line taking a second extensive inland detour, this time north of Helmsdale. Lybster itself is less than 25 miles from Helmsdale by the coast road, but the rail journey via Wick was just under 74 miles. However, it is no part of this review to speculate why the Highland main line north of Helmsdale did not take the coastal alternative. It may have been considered too expensive in terms of engineering at the time, but it did include rather more towns and villages to compensate by way of potential traffic and, as it was, the inland route was to prove tricky enough to build across the almost uninhabited heather and bog moors and the wastelands of Sutherland and Caithness - probably the remotest part of the whole of the British Isles.

In consequence, the Lybster line was built mainly to afford better travel facilities to some of those coastal settlements which would have been on a direct route from Helmsdale had it been built and also to give rail access to such places as depended on the quick despatch of perishable commodities such as fish - although the route south was circuitous, it did offer a valuable service for some 40 years in this role. Just as with the Dornoch branch, the line was authorised as a light railway, worked and part-financed by the Highland itself, but nominally independent until the grouping. It was opened in 1903 and represented the last significant element in the growth of the Highland Railway.

It is perhaps symptomatic of its local importance that it enjoyed near parity with the Wick and Thurso line in terms of passenger services and fared rather better in terms of freight

Unlike the line to Thurso, the Lybster branch did attract photographers during LMS days, from which it is clear that as with the Strathpeffer line, it too enjoyed a variety of motive power and rolling stock. This first view shows 'Yankee' 4-4-0T No.15013 about to depart from Lybster on 19th May 1928 with three six-wheelers. (The late H.C.Casserley)

A year or so later, No.15013, now devoid of smokebox numberplate but still in (rather grimy) red livery, is in charge of a mixed train at Lybster, the passenger portion now consisting of a relatively luxurious double-ended corridor composite brake of LNWR origin. (John Edgington Collection)

traffic frequency. Operated 'one engine in steam' from the terminus end as was customary (there was a small engine shed at Lybster), there were four regular trains per day in each direction during 1936: from Lybster at 7.50am, 12.27pm, 2.45pm and 5.50pm, returning from Wick at 11.20am, 1.20pm, 4.40pm and 7.15pm. This was actually a greater frequency than had existed in the earlier 1920s. Additionally, there was one extra morning train on Thursdays in both directions (8.50am from Wick; 10.00am from Lybster) along with a late evening Saturday only operation, again in both directions,

leaving Lybster at 9.30pm and not returning from Wick until 10.45pm. Of the regular daily trains, no fewer than three in each direction were officially regarded as 'mixed', the 1.20pm from Wick and 2.45pm from Lybster being the exceptions.

Somewhat surprisingly, the line was closed completely in April 1944 and later dismantled completely. It is thought that the improvement of the coast road by this time may have been a contributory factor, but its quick demise stands in sharp contrast to the somewhat similar Dornoch branch with which it shared many similarities.

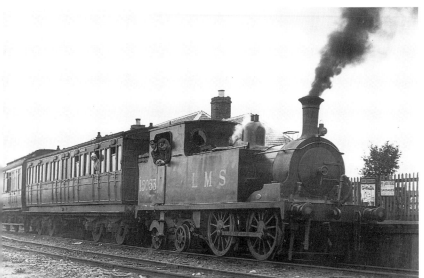

This is yet another operating cameo recorded by the late Henry Casserley, this time in July 1931. The Lybster branch is now in charge of a Peter Drummond 0-4-4T No.15053, first seen at the small engine shed preparing for duty, prior to taking its train to Wick, and then at the platform about to depart. The train is an ex-HR lavatory non-corridor composite, accompanied by another of the apparently ubiquitous ex-MR six-wheel clerestory full brakes which seem almost to have been mandatory in these parts during early LMS days. It is thought that the lady looking out of the carriage window is the photographer's wife.

In summer 1935, a rare visitor in the shape of Dugald Drummond ex-CR 0-4-4T, LMS No.15103, did a spell of duty between Wick and Lybster, probably standing in for one of the Highland locomotives during a period of works attention to the latter, the strong resemblance between the products of the Drummond brothers being readily apparent. Dugald's design was by far the older - built 1884, compared with 1905 for the Highland version. The train is a standard design LMS horsebox together with ex-Caledonian corridor composite brake.

(John Edgington Collection)

The Fort George Branch

This line, only 1.5 miles long, was the shortest of the Highland branches save for two half-mile goods only lines in the vicinity of Inverness not considered in this review - the Muirtown and Inverness Harbour branches. It was also the only branch from the Inverness-Keith route to enjoy anything like an extended life after the grouping.

The branch line replaced an older station on the Inverness to Nairn line which, although called Fort George, was about 3.5 miles from the military establishment from which it took its name. It was felt that the fort should have better rail access and this was duly authorised in 1890, though the line itself, across very easy terrain, was not opened until 1899. The older station, now a junction, was renamed Gollanfield, taking the name of a nearby farm.

*Fort George in March 1928
with the still almost new LMS
standard Class 3F 0-6-0T
No.16416 in charge. The train
is, unusually, of corridor
formation with a Highland
composite at the front and an
ex-LNWR third class behind
it. The full brake at the rear
cannot be positively identified
but could be of late Midland or
early LMS origin.*

(John Edgington Collection)

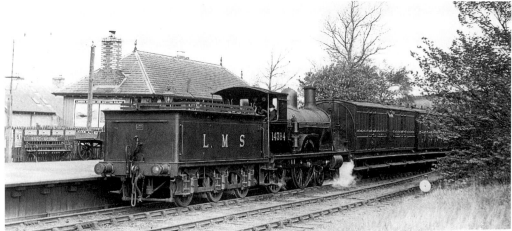

*Two years later, in May
1930, fairly fresh-painted
4-4-0 No.14394 Loch
Ashie was in charge of the
Fort George working. The
locomotive is in 1928 style
lined black LMS livery
and what can be seen of
the train shows two ex-HR
six-wheelers, both of them
now repainted in fully
lined LMS livery.*

(The late H.C.Casserley)

*Fort George in July 1931 now
offered 4-4-0 No.14398 Ben
Alder with a short train, the
leading vehicle being another
ubiquitous ex-MR clerestory
six-wheeler. The passenger
carriage is very probably a
composite but identification
is not really possible.*

(The late H.C.Casserley)

Alves, junction for the Hopeman branch, looking towards Inverness, date unknown. It was probably late LMS in view of the upper quadrant signal controlling entry to the branch in the distance and certainly taken after the branch was closed to passenger traffic. It displays the familiar 'twin gable plus colonnade' station building and the characteristic lattice footbridge. (M.Blakemore Collection)

This interesting view with the train crew clearly posing for the unknown photographer shows Hopeman in October 1926 with 4-4-0T No.15014 in charge of what is stated to be the 3.40pm mixed train to Alves. It contains the usual random mixture of carriage types to be found on most HR branches at the time: ex-MR six-wheel brake, ex-MR arc-roof six-wheel third, ex-HR six-wheel composite and a handful of goods wagons. (Peter Tatlow Collection)

When the new LMS standard 3F 0-6-0Ts arrived in the Inverness area, they were clearly not confined to yard shunting duties. This is No.16415, almost brand new, at Hopeman in May 1928 with a short train of which only the leading carriage can be positively identified - an ex-MR clerestory six-wheel brake, what else? What appears to be a goods van between the second coach and the final brake van, the latter of passenger-rated type, hints that it may have been officially classified as a mixed train. (The late H.C.Casserley)

During LMS days, services along the branch were pretty lavish in 1936, there being nine regular trains each day, shuttling between Fort George and Gollanfield from 8.25am (ex-Fort George) to 6.26pm (ex-Gollanfield). The majority of these made connections with the main line and, in addition, there were one or two extras on Wednesdays and Thursdays and a regular series of late night Saturday only workings, the last of them not leaving Gollanfield until 10.54pm. Journey time was only five minutes in either direction but there was plenty of work to keep the 'one engine in steam' occupied. As usual, it started and finished work at the terminus.

Freight traffic was handled by way of the ubiquitous mixed train of which five per day were officially listed in 1929 and thought to have operated for much of the LMS period. Two of them left Fort George at 8.25am and 2.25pm, but there were three in the reverse direction at 8.50am or 10.55am (depending on the day of the week), 2.50pm and 6.30pm.

Other than special military trains, passenger traffic ceased to operate in August 1943, but freight working continued for another fifteen years until well into the BR period.

The Hopeman Branch

This interesting line was the oldest of the Highland branches, having been promoted by the Inverness and Aberdeen Junction Railway and opened as far as the small village of Burghead in 1862. It also held the distinction of being the only branch line to have been opened before the incorporation of the Highland Railway itself in 1865. The branch was extended to Hopeman in 1892, at which time a new passenger station was provided at Burghead, the original terminus on the pier now becoming a goods only facility.

The Hopeman branch, along with its near-neighbour to Fochabers (below) was one of the first to lose part of its services in LMS days, passenger trains ceasing to run in 1931. Even towards the end, however, the LMS provided what was really quite a lavish service. The 1929 timetable lists ten trains per day in each direction, of which approximately half worked between Alves and Burghead only. Most of them made quite reasonable connections with main line services at Alves, the first train of the day leaving Hopeman at 8.00am and the last through train leaving Alves at 5.18pm with a later departure for Burghead only at 7.20pm. The majority of trains serving the full length of the line ran as mixed but by September 1929, the timetable lists five services as 'suspended'. Only two of these (one in each direction) had run the full length of the line.

At the end of the day, however, this area of Scotland was one of the first to suffer from serious bus competition and the closure of passenger services was unsurprising. By 1936, the LMS passenger timetables included the following note:

"The Train service on this Branch has been withdrawn. Parcels traffic will continue to be dealt with at Burghead and Hopeman. Frequent service of Omnibuses between Elgin, Hopeman and Burghead, for particulars of which see Local Omnibus Timetables."

The Hopeman branch continued in use for freight and parcels traffic until well into the BR period.

The Fochabers Branch

The idea of a branch to Fochabers was first mooted in the 1860s, a few years after the Inverness and Aberdeen Junction Railway had opened its main line to Keith. This line included a station called Fochabers but it was over four miles from the town by a not very direct road. Early proposals to build a branch line came to nought and it was not until 1893 that the Highland actually built the line. It started from the original main line station, renamed Orbliston Junction, and it finished on the west bank of the Spey. However, it was still some half a mile short of the town centre, it being felt too costly to bridge the river to get closer to the town itself.

This latter fact was the prime cause of its early loss of passenger services in 1931 at the same time as the Hopeman branch and for much the same reasons: competition from the more flexible omnibus. Prior to this, the rail service frequency was quite considerable, there being ten trains a day in each direction listed in the 1929 timetable, again mostly connecting with main line services. The first train of the day (mixed) left Fochabers at 6.45am and the last one (passenger) left Orbliston at 6.42pm. Only five trains (two from Fochabers and three in the reverse direction) were classified 'mixed' but by the end of 1929, like the Hopeman branch, some services were now listed in the timetable as 'suspended', two in each direction in this case. Freight and parcels traffic continued into BR days and the LMS 1936 passenger timetable carried the same sort of advisory note as quoted above for Hopeman.

The Portessie Branch

The final branch to be considered in this review was different from all the rest in two respects. Firstly, it did not run from the main line to a dedicated terminus and secondly, it was partially closed well before 1923 only to be partly re-opened again by the LMS during that year. It never carried passengers during LMS times but a brief note of its unique history will serve to round out the branch line story.

The branch was opened in 1884 to serve the farming district between Keith and the coast. It ran from a junction near Keith to the GNSR coastal line at Buckie, whence it ran parallel to the GNSR to Portessie where the Highland connected with the latter and used its station. It only remained in use until 1915 when the track between Aultmore and Buckie was lifted for use elsewhere - presumably to meet an urgent wartime need as it was intended to re-open the line after the war.

This was not considered urgent because traffic was unlikely to be heavy and it was not until the end of 1923 that track was relaid and preparations made for re-opening. However, neither passenger nor through trains returned, traffic never really prospered and eventually, the one time lucrative coastal fish traffic declined so much as to make even the HR station at Buckie unnecessary. The track was once again removed north of Aultmore, this time to Portessie itself (Buckie to Portessie closed completely in 1944) and the only portion to remain in use was the short stretch from Keith to Aultmore to serve the distillery at the latter place. This lasted well into BR days.

Fochabers Town station, May 1930 - 'Strath' Class 4-4-0 No.14274 Strathcarron *about to leave for Orbliston Junction with a two coach branch set: ex-MR full brake plus a former Highland composite. The locomotive displays a rather grimy 1928 style black livery, but whether lining is present cannot be stated. Another view of this train arriving at the junction on the same day will be found in Chapter 2.* (The late H.C.Casserley)

The abandoned station at Buckie, date unspecified, from which it can be seen that the facilities provided had been quite lavish when the line was open. The view is towards Portessie, the route from Keith entering from behind the camera position and veering right to run parallel with the GNSR just beyond the station. (The late Gavin Wilson Collection)

This view of Portessie station, taken in 1937, shows the disused ex-Highland line on the right and the GNSR main line on the left. The two converged just beyond the buildings in the far distance. This picture clearly shows the somewhat bleak and unrewarding nature of the surrounding area as far as traffic potential was concerned. (The late Gavin Wilson Collection)

Locomotives and Rolling Stock

LOCOMOTIVES

At the grouping, the Highland Railway had developed a highly distinctive fleet of locomotives, some 173 in total, of which 23 were withdrawn before their 1923 LMS numbers were allotted. Most of these were elderly 'Crewe Type' 4-4-0s - see also the footnote to Table IX which lists the remaining Highland types in their new number order viz: Passenger tender (14XXX); Passenger tank (15XXX); Freight tank (16XXX); Freight tender (17XXX). In each block, locomotives were arranged by ascending wheel arrangement in their newly assessed LMS power class (lowest first), gaps in the number sequence being explained by the fact that in 1923, the LMS put all its inherited Scottish types into one consolidated Northern Division number series regardless of originating company. However, specific locomotive classes (save for odd mistakes) were kept together by running numbers, whilst within any one power category, the order of numbering Scottish types was CR; G&SWR; HR.

TABLE IX: HIGHLAND LOCOMOTIVES INHERITED BY THE LMS

Description and type	Quantity	LMS numbers/Power Class
Jones 'Strath' Class 4-4-0	6	14271-6, Class 1 later 1P *
Jones 'Skye Bogie' Class 4-4-0	1	14277, Class 1, later 1P *
Jones 'Bruce' Class 4-4-0	1	14278, Class 1, later 1P *
Jones 'Skye Bogie' Class 4-4-0	7	14279-85, Class 1 later 1P *
Jones 'Loch' Class 4-4-0	18	14379-96, Class 2, later 2P
Drummond 'Small Ben' Class 4-4-0	20	14397-416, Class 2, later 2P
Drummond 'Large Ben' Class 4-4-0	6	14417-22, Class 2 later 2P
Cumming 4-4-0	2	14522-3, Class 3, later 3P
Drummond 'Castle' Class 4-6-0	19	14675-93, Class 3, later 3P
Cumming 'Clan' Class 4-6-0	8	14762-9, Class 4, later 4P
Jones 4-4-0T	3	15010-2, Unclassed *
'Yankee' 4-4-0T	5	15013-7, Unclassed
Jones 0-4-4T	1	15050, Unclassed, later 0P
Drummond 0-4-4T	4	15051-4, Unclassed, later 0P
Drummond 0-6-4T	8	15300-7, Class 4, later 4P
Stroudley 0-6-0T	3	16118-8/16383, Unclassed
Drummond 0-6-0T	3	16380-2, Class 2, later 2F
Drummond 0-6-0	12	17693-704, Class 3, later 3F
Jones 'Goods' 4-6-0	15	17916-30, Class 4, later 4F
Cumming 'Clan Goods' 4-6-0	8	17950-7, Class 4, later 4F

* **Footnote:** These were the survivors which displayed the 'Crewe Type' front end treatment (ie continuous wrapper round smokebox and outside cylinders) and will be referred to as such throughout this chapter.

For the record, the so-called 'Yankee' 4-4-0Ts were not designed by the Highland CME at the time, David Jones, but were contractor-built in 1892 for use in Uruguay and, in the end, purchased by the HR. Two mistakes were made in the renumbering series and never subsequently rectified. 'Skye Bogie' No.14277 was numbered out of proper sequence in the mistaken belief that it was another 'Bruce' Class survivor, whilst the Stroudley 0-6-0T No.16383 was wrongly identified as being one of the Drummond 0-6-0Ts, the latter often being referred to as 'Scrap' tanks having been assembled in 1903 at Lochgorm, using mostly recovered parts, including boilers, from dismantled 2-4-0 locomotives.

Fortunately, the Highland locomotive fleet has been well covered both in pre-group and LMS days (see bibliography), so there is no need to give any further details than are summarised above. Moreover, most of them feature in at least one of the many pictures in this book for those who are less familiar with the many variations in style and livery. Far more interesting in the LMS context is the high rate of survival of many classes after 1922 and the reasons behind it. To make this point more clearly, I have prepared Table X to show the rate of reduction of the Highland fleet at four yearly intervals during LMS days. This disguises some of the intermediate changes but does give an accurate overview.

TABLE X: HIGHLAND LOCOMOTIVES - NUMBERS IN SERVICE AT THE START OF EACH YEAR LISTED

Description	1924	1928	1932	1936	1940	1944	1948
'Strath' 4-4-0	6	5			(Extinct 1930)		
'Skye Bogie' 4-4-0	8	5			(Extinct 1930)		
'Bruce' 4-4-0	1	1			(Extinct 1930)		
'Loch' 4-4-0	18	18	18	11	7	4	2
'Small Ben' 4-4-0	20	20	19	17	15	15	10
'Large Ben' 4-4-0	6	6	6	2	(Extinct 1937)		
Cumming 4-4-0	2	2	2	1	(Extinct 1936)		
'Castle' 4-6-0	19	19	18	15	9	8	(Ext't 1947)
'Clan' 4-6-0	8	8	8	8	8	7	2
Jones 4-4-0T	3	3	1		(Extinct 1932)		
'Yankee' 4-4-0T	5	2	2		(Extinct 1934)		
Jones 0-4-4T	1	1			(Extinct 1929)		
Drummond 0-4-4T	4	4	3	3	3	3	2
Drummond 0-6-4T	8	8	8	1	(Extinct 1936)		
Stroudley 0-6-0T	3	1	1		(Extinct 1932)		
Drummond 0-6-0T	3	3	1		(Extinct 1932)		
Drummond 0-6-0	12	12	12	12	11	11	7
'Jones Goods' 4-6-0	15	15	13	7	1	(Extinct 1940*)	
'Clan Goods' 4-6-0	8	8	8	8	8	8	6
Totals	**150**	**141**	**120**	**85**	**62**	**56**	**29**

* Prototype (HR 103 - LMS 17916) preserved by LMS in 1934

Drummond 0-6-0T No.16382 seen at Perth in May 1928 carrying the first version of the LMS freight livery. These were the so-called 'Scrap' tanks - see text - and all three had been withdrawn by the end of 1932.

(The late H.C.Casserley)

Left: Many former Highland locomotives carried visible signs of post-grouping alterations in the form of new standardised works plates. This one is typical, having been attached to 4-4-0 No.14406 Ben Slioch in 1927. Note that the work was carried out at Kilmarnock, at which time the locomotive would almost certainly have received a replacement CR boiler - hence the 'rebuilt' wording.

(The late H.C.Casserley)

Below: Jones 4-4-0T No.15010 was the very last of the 'Crewe Type' Highland locomotives to be withdrawn, surviving until 1932, some two to three years after its two sister engines and all the similar tender types had gone. It is seen here shunting at Inverness in 1931. (Gordon Coltas)

Above: Jones 0-4-4T No.15050 was the only one of its kind to reach the LMS. Seen here in LMS crimson livery at Wick shed in May 1928, it was used on the Lybster branch until it was withdrawn in 1929. (The late H.C.Casserley)

In 1928, an unexpected visitor to Inverness was seen in the shape of ex-Midland Kirtley 2-4-0 No.4. The reasons for its presence are somewhat obscure, but one possibility is that it may have been an attempt to find a replacement for some of the older Highland classes. If so, it was a very peculiar choice, given that it was older than most of them and was itself withdrawn in 1930. This view, taken on 21st May 1928 at Inverness shed, shows it in company with an equally venerable Jones 'Strath' Class 4-4-0 No.14271 Sir George. (The late H.C.Casserley)

The first point to note is that totals remained static until 1924, and even after this only nine engines were taken out of service during the first four years of LMS ownership, not all of which were the venerable Crewe Types either. Four years later, the grand total had still only declined by a modest 20% compared with 1923, but by now almost all the older and smaller engines had gone and by 1934, only three Drummond 0-4-4Ts survived from this once fascinating group of classes - they lasted manfully until the end of WWII and two reached BR: they had a specific role which will be addressed below. Meantime, the next eight years from 1932 to 1940 were to see a major change in the withdrawal pattern which resulted in a virtual halving of the HR fleet, followed by another halving again by 1948.

So much for raw statistics, but what do they reveal of LMS policy at the time? Once again risking the implicit danger of making broad generalisations, the basic story seems to me to fall into three distinct phases, albeit a bit blurred at the transition points between them.

One of the first three LMS standard types to be drafted into the Highland section was the Class 3F 0-6-0T. They were used mainly for yard shunting at Inverness and No.7333 was on this duty in July 1937.

(John Edgington Collection)

The first ten years

The first ten years of locomotive evolution on the Highland Section of the LMS were dominated by the principles already outlined in Chapter 1 - ie the quasi-standardisation of basic Caledonian precepts pending a wider introduction of new LMS standard types. Quite apart from the already noted similarity between many of the HR classes and those of the CR, this idea would not have been too unacceptable at Inverness, for the last CME of the Highland, David C.Urie, took over as Mechanical Engineer, LMS Northern Division, soon after the grouping and was himself instrumental in the fitting of Caledonian type boilers to Highland locomotives.

It can therefore be no surprise that the larger HR classes, both physically and numerically, survived almost wholly intact (with one or two exceptions) during this first ten years. What is perhaps more interesting is that many smaller and older classes enjoyed a rather remarkable stay of execution when set against LMS policy in general. The several Crewe Types dominated in this respect, though not exclusively so, and the LMS clearly found plenty for them to do. In part this may have been in consequence of their lighter axle loading, their principal, albeit not exclusive, haunts in early LMS days being on the Kyle line (from which route, of course, the small-wheeled Skye Bogies had derived their popular name) and on the many branches, the latter being often the final resting places for the larger-wheeled Strath and Bruce type 4-4-0s.

What does seem clear is that the gradual upgrading of many routes to take heavier locomotives, combined with the full or partial closure of some of the branch lines in the early 1930s - see Chapter 4 - prompted the final withdrawal of almost all these physically smaller types save for the aforementioned Drummond 0-4-4Ts which remained in use. This was because of the peculiar 'light railway' status of the Wick and Lybster and Dornoch branches - again see Chapter 4 - where light axle loading remained essential. Here, the Drummond tanks were kept in use after all the older lightweight types had gone - usually two working (one on each branch) and one in reserve.

They were retained on these jobs until the Lybster branch was closed, after which one of them was withdrawn. The other two remained on call for duties between The Mound and Dornoch until well into BR days until they were finally replaced by, of all things, GWR design 0-6-0 pannier tanks!

During this first phase, the introduction of new LMS types was slow to non-existent, mostly confined to Inverness and south thereof and, as far as can be judged, only involved three types, dominantly tender designs. This itself perpetuated a strong Highland tradition of using tender engines for almost everything save pure yard shunting and merits a degree of amplification. Many Highland duties involved quite lengthy trips where the extra coal and water capacity of tender types was often of vital importance. Moreover, because of the nature of the line itself - see Chapter 2 - Highland locomotives rarely had very large driving wheels and the 'mixed traffic' concept was adopted in fact if not in name long before it became a far more widespread national practice: there was no real 'horses for courses' philosophy north of Perth, despite the many named engines and the proliferation of LMS red livery after 1922....

It can therefore be no surprise that the first LMS standard 'imports' were seven Midland-derived Class 4F 0-6-0s in 1927, followed by ten Horwich mixed traffic Class 5P4F 2-6-0s (aka 'Crabs') in 1928, both of which types were well at home on any task to which they might be allocated, given the absence of any need for really high speed operation. The 2-6-0s very quickly settled down on the main line via Slochd, but were excluded from the Dava route and other sections of the Highland. The 4Fs were more widespread but did not find too much favour. To these were added four MR-style Class 3F 0-6-0Ts, mostly put to use for yard shunting at Inverness and Forres, where they replaced the elderly Stroudley 0-6-0Ts, plus a bit of branch line working - and that was just about it....

Meantime, banking duty from Blair Atholl to Druimuachdar (and to a lesser extent between Forres and Dava) remained the almost exclusive preserve and main task for the impressive

Peter Drummond six-coupled tanks at Blair Atholl. In the first picture, ex-HR 0-6-4T No.15307 is seen in red livery in May 1928 and would have been on routine banking duty. The lower view shows the visually similar 0-6-2T design which Drummond introduced onto the G&SWR after his move to Kilmarnock from the Highland. These locomotives were more numerous than their HR ancestors, numbered in the freight tank series and painted plain black as seen here on No.16907 c.1936. This was one of ten engines ordered in Drummond's time but not built until Whitelegg had taken over on the G&SWR. They were similar in appearance to the original Drummond version save for a slightly modified cab opening and larger tank capacity.

(The late H.C.Casserley; Author's collection)

Drummond 0-6-4Ts for many years, the engines staying intact as a class during the whole of this first phase. Surprisingly, the LMS classified them as passenger types and painted them red from 1923-8, unlike their newer and similar G&SWR 0-6-2T cousins, also by Peter Drummond, always regarded as goods types, being given a black livery in consequence. In due course, two of the latter engines replaced some of the 0-6-4Ts at Blair Atholl on what was one of the few tank engine jobs on the Highland outwith yard duty.

This first phase also saw the beginnings of a bit of cross-posting of pre-group types in Scotland. Precise details are not easy to determine with accuracy as to 'which locomotives and when', but one transfer which does merit comment is that of the ex-Caledonian 'River' Class 4-6-0s to the Highland lines after the grouping. This design by W.M.Smith was initiated by the Highland in 1915 but rejected by the civil engineers, after

the engines were built, on the grounds of excess axle weight, thus enabling the CR to purchase a fine clutch of six engines 'off the peg' which were better than anything it had available at the time. By a fine stroke of irony, these locomotives came back to the Highland at much the same time as the standard 4Fs and 2-6-0s first appeared (above); but even more ironic, must have been the later transfer of all the Highland Clans and two Castles to the Caledonian's Oban line in replacement of the markedly inferior McIntosh and Pickersgill 4-6-0s. Some of the Clans later came back to the Highland Section.

Whatever, gradual civil engineering improvements across the whole of the Highland network, especially on the Far North and Kyle lines, undoubtedly paved the way for heavier engines to be used north of Inverness and this had two effects. Firstly, it allowed the withdrawal of many older light axle-load types

The 'River' Class 4-6-0s - see text - came back onto the Highland lines at much the same time as the first of the LMS standard types appeared. Here, No.14757 (originally intended to be HR No.71 River Spey*) is seen at Perth shed in 1930, still wearing the pre-1928 crimson livery.*

(Gordon Coltas)

Above and left: Reverse transfers. By the later 1930s, two of the former HR 4-6-0 designs were finding plenty to do on the Caledonian's 'Oban Road'. The first picture shows 'Castle' Class No.14686 Urquart Castle *at Oban in 1937 while the next view shows 'Clan' Class No.14768* Clan McKenzie *taking water at Luib in August 1938. Carriage enthusiasts might like to note that the leading coach (ex-LNWR double-ended brake composite) still carries the fully lined LMS livery, officially superseded some four years earlier.*

(Peter Tatlow Collection; Author's collection)

The Stanier Class 3P 2-6-2Ts did not stay long on the Highland section and this rare view shows No.185 on local passenger duty at Grantown on Spey in April 1938. The train is an ex-LNWR brake composite and note that the locomotive is still fitted with a snowplough.

(The late Gavin Wilson)

which had been kept going for some time, as already explained above, but secondly, it also permitted a simultaneous transfer of larger and more powerful ex-HR types to serve these routes, thus paving the way for the major insertion of new standard LMS types south of Inverness. And it to this which I now turn.

The middle LMS years: c.1933-40

Perusal of Table X will reveal that between 1933 and 1940, not only was there a total clear-out of some of the older and less numerous residual Highland classes, relatively unscathed until then, but also a marked reduction in the number of survivors of even those types whose lives had been prolonged by fitting them with CR-type boilers &c. The answer was quite simple: the introduction of the Stanier LMS standard Class 5 4-6-0.

Stanier came to the LMS as CME in 1932 and what many see as his finest design of locomotive in terms of the total needs of the railway was introduced in 1934. Although its initial effect on the Highland is to some extent disguised by the specific four-year intervals adopted in Table X, some of the first examples were sent immediately to Perth in 1934 and, almost equally quickly, began to have a profound effect. It is no exaggeration to say that they could do just about anything which was required of them on the system and their pet name 'Hikers' (ie go anywhere and do anything), adopted only on the Highland lines as far as I am aware, just about summed it up. They were, in effect, a perfect solution for the Highland lines in the context of the later 1930s.

In fairly short order they took over most of the principal expresses and long distance freight hauls, albeit sometimes assisted by older types when double-heading was appropriate. In this latter regard, the Highland never really changed and

double heading was always very common. Indeed, it even went so far as to provide double sets of water columns at many of the intermediate stations so that both train engines could replenish their tanks simultaneously. Even so, the Class 5s were less in need of assistance than their predecessors and it seems very significant to this writer that from their very first appearance on the scene, if photographic evidence is any guide, they regularly operated on their own. They also saw off the bulk of the earlier LMS standard types too: there were relatively few 'Crabs' or 4F 0-6-0s on Highland lines after the Class 5s came on the scene, although some did remain.

Tempting though it would be to wax lyrical about the effect of this outstanding design, suffice to say, as Table X reveals, that the Class 5 4-6-0 was the means whereby the residual ex-HR fleet (despite its generally high quality given its age) was halved in only eight years and it is interesting to see what was actually left in 1940. The residual Lochs and most Small Bens were still available for lighter duties (and/or piloting), but all the Clans had now gone to the Oban line (see above), plus at least two Castles. Meantime, the Clan Goods had taken over many significant workings on the Kyle and Far North lines and the Drummond 0-6-0s (affectionately known as 'Barneys' for some obscure reason) were still almost 100% intact for local goods tasks and piloting. All the Drummond 0-6-4Ts had now gone, though this was a case where Class 5s could not and did not substitute(!), and the only new shunting engines north of Perth were LMS standard Class 3F 0-6-0Ts: all change indeed.

But the Class 5 could not do everything, of course, hence the survival of some older types - eg the Drummond 0-4-4Ts mentioned above. And some interesting developments had also taken place. In 1939, five Stanier 2-6-2Ts were sent to Blair Atholl to take over much of the work, though they were hardly suited for banking duty and were sent to Glasgow in 1940. But a year earlier, two of them were sent to Aviemore for working locals to Grantown and Forres - arguably one of the first if not the very first example of tank engine working on the main line. It is not known how long they remained there, but the Blair Atholl allocation was replaced by Caledonian design 0-4-4Ts. During the 1930s, these excellent engines, made redundant by new LMS types in their former territory, took over many of the Highland branch duties and the Aberfeldy branch in particular became their almost exclusive preserve.

These were not the only imports, however, mention having already been made of Peter Drummond's ex-G&SWR 0-6-2Ts taking over from some of his earlier Highland 0-6-4Ts on banking duties at Blair Atholl. Likewise, the relatively elderly status of most Highland 0-6-0Ts - few enough when all is said and done - caused not only LMS Class 3F 0-6-0Ts to take their place in due course, but also led to a few ex-CR 0-6-0Ts and 0-4-0STs to be transferred to Inverness, the latter to work the harbour branch. Similarly, ex-CR 4-4-0s of both superheated Dunalastair IV and Pickersgill styles, displaced by newer types on their native metals, began to take over some jobs from less powerful and older Highland types. These later imports were vaguely similar to the displaced ex-HR types in many ways, of course, and continued to serve the Highland well into BR days.

82

Wartime and afterwards

There seems to be but little doubt that had not WWII taken place, the remainder of the Highland locomotive fleet would have been despatched to the scrapyard as quickly as had taken place between 1932 and 1940. But as things happened, the last eight years of LMS ownership were to see the scrapping rate reduced to 1924-32 levels. Apart from the solitary remaining Jones Goods 4-6-0 (withdrawn in 1940), some members of all the other residual Highland classes survived the war and only one type became extinct, the Castle 4-6-0 - and even this was not until April 1947.

The reasons are not hard to seek. As in WWI, albeit not perhaps quite to the same degree of intensity, the Highland line became an essential artery for vital supplies to the Far North in support of the fleet at Scapa Flow. This inevitably posed the need to keep every locomotive operational if it could 'turn a wheel in anger', so to speak, just as it did in many other parts of the country for that matter. In consequence, engines were only withdrawn if they were totally beyond redemption. Many of them could be given a few more years against this sort of scenario and one or two ex-HR locomotives were patched up and reinstated after formal withdrawal. Some new locomotives were, of course, put into service during those hard times, but many of these were for overseas use and the programme was strictly regulated by Government.

It is therefore not surprising, as can be seen from Table X, that by far the majority of HR survivors in 1940 also lasted out the war years. Thereafter, as things gradually returned to what passed for normal in the later 1940s, the scrapping rate was to increase again as Class 5s took over the Kyle and Far North lines. To be strictly accurate, this type had been seen north of Inverness before the war but it never dominated as it did on other Highland routes at the same time.

Meantime, some LMS standard Class 8F 2-8-0s and Class 4 2-6-4Ts of Stanier and Fairburn design also began to be seen, the latter being especially well liked in Scotland after the war. The 8Fs arrived during the war and were an attempt to avoid double heading, in which they well and truly succeeded. Speed was not a priority but they did improve running times. Some eighteen of them were allocated to Perth in 1944, there being many stories of them hauling prodigious loads 'over The Hill'. All had left the Highlands well before 1948 to be replaced by Class 5 4-6-0s, the latter being far more flexible in the duties to which they could be allocated under normal conditions.

The Fairburn 2-6-4s went to Scotland from 1945 mainly to replace many older passenger tanks in the suburban role - eg the ex-CR 0-4-4Ts in the Glasgow area. However, some were also used on the Kyle line in 1946 while the turntable there was being renewed (hence their presence at Inverness), but did not stay thereafter. A batch was, however, allocated to Blair Atholl for banking duties. Even so, notwithstanding these and the ex-CR 'imports' mentioned earlier, there were still 29 of the original Highland engines in service when BR took over.

The majority of these did not last too much longer and few received their allotted BR numbers. Of those which did, the

---

A panoramic view of part of the busy Inverness yards in 1937. Amongst many details which may be noted are a pair of ex-CR 0-6-0Ts (unidentified) on shunting duty, a typical Highland goods brake van in the left foreground behind the trees and a relatively high proportion of covered goods vans. Modellers of the late 1930s period should find this picture especially helpful in terms of both the types and variety of rolling stock featured.   (Peter Tatlow Collection)

two surviving Drummond 0-4-4Ts (LMS Nos.15051/3) merit a special mention as the last of the Highland breed (lasting until 1956/7); how nice it would have been to see either one of them preserved. As it was, however, and despite a valiant attempt to keep the last Small Ben for posterity (LMS No.14398, ex-HR No.2 *Ben Alder* and allocated BR No.54398), it was finally scrapped and only the pioneering Jones Goods 4-6-0 remains to remind us of a once noteworthy fleet of fine locomotives. As with the residual preserved engines from the other four pre-group companies north of the border, it does not seem to me to be anything like an adequate representation of the significant Scottish contribution to British locomotive history.

Two former Caledonian locomotive types which were familiar in the Highlands during LMS days. The first picture shows a Dugald Drummond 0-4-0ST No.16011 at Inverness in 1939 - note the diminutive shunters' truck which often accompanied these locomotives. The second undated picture, but almost certainly taken during 1947-8, features the superheated McIntosh 'Dunalastair IV' Class 4-4-0 No.14363 in the sort of typical utility unlined black wartime livery which many of these engines carried until BR style took over. Both of the engines featured survived until BR times but 14363 did not last beyond 1948.

(Peter Tatlow Collection - 2)

Although superficially featuring locomotives, these two pictures, both taken at Inverness, are probably of more interest now in terms of the coaching stock in the background. In the first view, taken in 1930, 'River' Class 4-6-0 No.14757 and LMS 2-6-0 No.13107 are seen backing down to the station and partially hiding a fascinating set of LNER carriages. The exact types cannot be identified with precision but Gresley (LNER and/or GNR), NBR and GNSR styles seem to be represented, while the clerestory dining car just to the left of the 2-6-0's tender can only be ex-NER or ex-GER.

In the second picture, taken a year later, an immaculately presented No.14395 Loch Garve in lined black 1928 livery was undoubtedly the reason for taking the picture. But in the background can be seen a unique clerestory dining car of G&SWR origin, transferred to the Highland section after 1923 and used on services north of Inverness. (Gordon Coltas - 2)

ROLLING STOCK

Unlike locomotives, whose many ramifications have been set down in print almost *ad nauseam*, regardless of their original owning company, the matter of rolling stock (without which there would be no need for locomotives at all - sic!) is far less comprehensively recorded - and the Highland Railway was no exception. It is therefore impossible to offer more than a basic overview of the situation which the LMS inherited in 1923, based on such information as has survived. What can be said, of course, is that the HR contribution to the LMS carriage and wagon fleet was so numerically insignificant as to have had no influence at all in the design of what followed - LMS standard

carriage and wagon practice (based on Midland ideas with some LNWR input) reigned supreme after 1922.

To be fair, this was to result in some very considerable improvements in passenger amenity north of the border, not least in the Highlands, but this is not to say that what did remain of the Highland fleet was totally unimportant. It took time for changes to take place, of course, and for quite some time, the continued existence of some elements of its modest vehicle collection (generally remaining mostly confined to its original 'home' territory) was to add a welcome element of variety to the LMS scene.

Carriages and 'Passenger Rated' Stock

Perusal of the LMS 1923 renumbering list for carriage stock reveals that ex-Highland passenger carrying coaches amounted to fewer than 300 (LMS Nos.18591-864). This may not seem many, but viewed against the size of the system at the time (not to mention that a serious attempt to get rid of older six-wheel types had already started, believed to be because there was no longer any real need for such vehicles on long distance service), this modest total was probably more than adequate for purely local purposes. Most of the better stock which came to the LMS was of bogie type, the bulk of it built in the early 20th Century and not very different in concept from most other carriages of the time, no matter what company, save for trivial and unimportant cosmetic differences so beloved of enthusiasts and which some of the accompanying views show.

The HR fleet also included a handful of agreeable corridor types for through services south of Perth, plus a fair number of lavatory non-corridors for longer distance local use. Given that these domestic types were often augmented by a multiplicity of through carriages (often luxurious) which found their way onto the Highland lines from many parts of the rest of the British system south of Perth, it will be seen that passenger amenities offered on the Highland main lines were regularly more attractive than a mere study of the basic HR carriage fleet in isolation might suggest - and the LMS was not slow to take this idea forward as it began to insert additional corridor and dining cars onto the scene.

Not all were exactly brand new, especially the dining cars, but all were of high quality and such was the rate of production of new LMS standard 'ordinary' stock that some of the newer types, both corridor and non-corridor, soon migrated north and were used to a far wider extent on relatively minor services than may often be supposed: and soon into the new régime for that matter. There is, for example, pictorial evidence of an LMS corridor brake composite of mid-1920s vintage in service between Wick and Lybster in the early 1930s - not bad for such a remote line and certainly worthy of comment; and it was by no means unique. Even in later days, the Dornoch line was served by quite modern LMS types to the very end.

On the whole, therefore, rather than try to analyse a very complex situation from what limited official information has survived, I have preferred to deal with this section of the story by way of offering as many pictures as space will allow in this and previous chapters, together with as much caption detail as I am able to provide.

Turning now to Non-Passenger Coaching Stock, this was an area where the Highland, compared with its passenger carrying fleet, owned even more vehicles. There was always an element of 'blurring at the edges' when it came to defining the exact difference between NPCS and the better fully fitted freight stock of the time, but almost 500 ex-HR vehicles were thus identified in 1923, and given LMS NPCS Nos.7361-848. Over half were renumbered from goods stock, which indicates the nature of the problem, and there were some 300 fish trucks in the total. However defined, this was a far higher proportion of NPCS (related to the whole) than most if not all other British companies could offer and reflected the considerable use of such vehicles in the Highlands - a fact already discussed to some extent in Chapter 3.

These pictures show three characteristic Highland bogie carriage designs which survived to reach the LMS, viz:

Opposite: Arc-roof fully panelled lavatory third class No.18997 (in the 1933 carriage number series), still in full livery c.1936.

Right, above: Arc-roof matchboard-style lavatory composite No.19985 in what looks like unlined utility red livery at Aviemore in 1946. There has been a bit of transfer replacement - note the post-war style flat-topped '3s' on three of the doors.

Right, below: This low-elliptical roof matchboard-style corridor third No.3395, taken from the corridor side, was seen in simplifed 1934 style LMS carriage livery at Inverness.

(Peter Tatlow Collection - 2; Gavin Wilson)

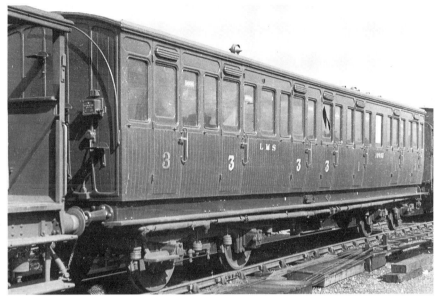

Freight Stock

Despite the crucial economic importance of freight traffic to the LMS, already mentioned in earlier chapters, the final part of this section of the survey is, in purely space terms, by far the shortest. This is unfortunate, for I have no doubt that much more could be said if only the evidence had survived. But no matter how important it may have been to the company, it has to be said that freight train working attracted little attention from contemporary observers or photographers for that matter,

Arguably the two most-photographed Highland freight vehicle designs are represented here by double-deck sheep van No.294528 and six-wheel guard's brake van No.294071. Note the double doors on the latter.

(Peter Tatlow Collection)

on the latter of whom we rely so much for visual evidence. In addition, far less original research has been carried out in this field as far as the actual *modus operandi* was concerned, much less the vehicles which actually did the job.

A further problem with freight traffic is that the vehicles in any one freight formation rarely reflected (proportionally) the company over which it was running. By the time the LMS got into its stride, many company-owned freight vehicles (save for highly specialised 'non-common user' types) were used by all companies on a sort of 'quid pro quo' basis regardless of who owned them or where they may have ended up, so the fact that in 1923, the Highland passed fewer than 3,000 goods vehicles to the LMS does not really mean anything. It merely reflects the relative size of the HR compared with other companies.

Highland goods vehicles were mostly conventional in form and neither better nor worse than their contemporaries from other companies. The balance between merchandise types was much as found elsewhere in the country - ie a high proportion of open wagons and few covered vans. There were not many mineral wagons, save for loco coal, but there were quite a few timber wagons and cattle/sheep vans. As for their use, it is impossible to come up with generalisations which will add meaning to the nature of freight services during LMS days, when any sort of freight vehicles from any part of the country could well turn up on Highland metals.

That said, it might be worth mentioning that the Highland's goods brake vans, which rarely if ever left their 'home' system, often had their own distinctive 'architecture', including the raised 'birdcage' lookout in many cases. They also lacked the open verandahs often found elsewhere in the country. This was because they often served as 'road vans' carrying 'smalls' traffic and in consequence, were longer than those used by many other railways and had two sets of double doors. The familiar 'double deck' sheep vans were also rather characteristic and it is probably for this reason that these two types were just about the only really well photographed Highland goods vehicles.